W9-CUO-836

Wow! Where do I even start when talking about Tony Kellar? Tony has been a vital part of my outfitting business! Tony's wide array of outdoor knowledge paired with his amazing culinary ability make him one of the finest gourmet river guides I have ever come across. Everyone who is interested in exploring the outdoors will benefit from reading this book. This is an enjoyable and informative read for even the most seasoned of outdoorsmen and women.

Chad Cadwell
Owner Operator Missouri River Expeditions

"Camping and Cooking WithThe Bare Essentials is an "essential" tool for anyone who is trying to concoct the perfect combination of outdoors know-how, kitchen savvy and outdoor splendor. A "must have" for any aspiring outdoor gourmet cook!"

Denise Blomberg,
Outdoor Women of South Dakota

"Tony is a culinary connoisseur masquerading as a river guide! I am always amazed at the amount of fantastic food that he can pack into a kayak. Some of the highlights of our kayaking trips are waking up to the smells of coffee and breakfast cooking over an open camp fire, and then ending the day with one of Tony's famous Gourmet wonders."

Dan Coffey

Camping & Cooking

With the Bare Essentials

Your Complete Guide to Easier Camping and Gourmet Outdoor Cooking

FOUR WINDS PUBLISHING

A division of North Country Enterprises
P.O. Box 65
Mission Hill, SD 57046

At North Country Enterprises we don't just cook, we create.
We don't just teach, we foster growth and experience.
We don't just guide, we host.

www.gonorthcountry.org

Copyright © 2004 Tony Kellar

Illustrations by Scott Luken
P.O. Box 159 • Yankton, SD 57078

Cover and text design by
Donna Bollich • Fordyce, NE

Edited by
Mary Johnson

Back page photo of author by
Personal Touch Photography

All rights reserved. No part of this book may be used or
reproduced in any manner whatsoever without written
permission of the publisher.

Four Winds authors are available for seminars and speaking
engagements. If interested please contact us at the address listed above.

ATTENTION: SCHOOLS, BUSINESSES AND ORGANIZATIONS
Four Winds books are available at quantity discounts with
bulk purchase for educational, business or promotional use.
For more information, contact:
Four Winds Publishing
P.O. Box 65
Mission Hill, SD 57046

ISBN 0-9753016-0-8

Printed in the United States of America

First Edition: March 2004

10 9 8 7 6 5 4

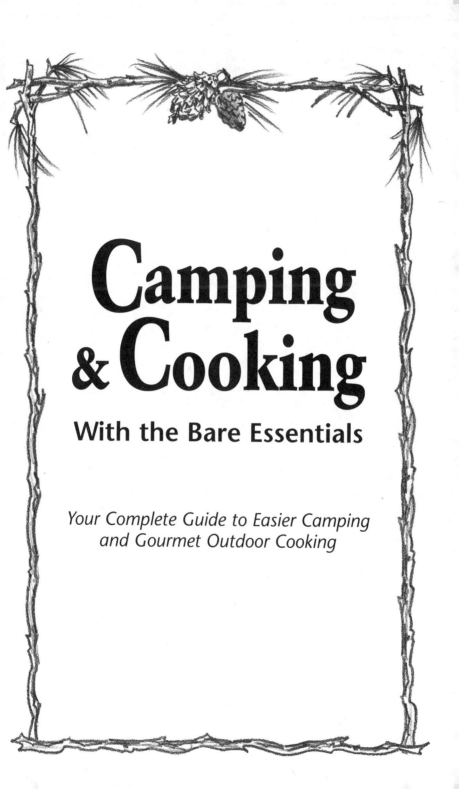

Camping & Cooking

With the Bare Essentials

*Your Complete Guide to Easier Camping
and Gourmet Outdoor Cooking*

Special thanks!

I would like to extend the most sincere thanks to everyone who has helped me along the trail.

First of all – to the River Rats: Dad, Ed, Pat, Josh, you guys inspire me.

Thanks Mom and Dad, Brandy, Tristan and Josh.

Love and pride to my son, T.J.

A big thanks to Chad Cadwell for his support, encouragement, and friendship. Also to R.J., Matt, Matty and all of the other guides at Missouri River Expeditions – "Paddle on." To MRE alumni all over ... thanks for sharing your experiences with me on the river.

South Dakota Outdoor Womens Association – thanks so much for the helping hand, the good times, and the past and future paddles. Special thanks to Denise and Susie.

Special warm thank you's to the best crew ever at the Shamrock bar – you guys rock the house (Wooly Bully!!)

Big thanks go to the Rick and Mary Hurd family, to the "Rattlesnake" Harry and Linda Walters family, and to Mike Miller and his family for the hospitality, opportunity, and friendship. Not to mention the good hunting and for the opportunity to share their little slices of heaven along the Missouri River.

Also a big thanks to Jacks Canoe rental in Spooner, Wisconsin.

This book could have never happened without the support and help from Paul Lowrie, Scott Luken and of course – the dynamic duo of Mary Johnson and Donna Bollich.

And credit for the cover photo (and more than I can ever say) has to go to one of the nicest, most beautiful people in the world, with whom I'll always share a deep and wonderful friendship, Trudi Olmanson.

Thanks Grandma Mary, for helping with initial edits, and for being the sweet lady you are.

And thank you so much Grandpa Norman for teaching me about the hunt.

For tech support, computer solutions, late night brews, and great friendship – thanks to Lance Corbit.

God bless all my family and friends, here and passed.

TABLE OF CONTENTS

Preface:

It's been said that camping requires only one meal per day. It begins when you wake up and ends right before bed in the evening. This is a pretty accurate statement, from where I sit.

It seems that the days could be divided into time-slots between snacks and meals. And many would agree that food never tasted so good as when you spent the day hiking, canoeing, climbing, or even just sitting out in the forest.

Fresh air and sunshine seem to be culinary aphrodisiacs for me. The welcome, familiar smell of a beacon campfire and a picnic table, or a spot in the grass, are my ambiance. Countless stars winking in the summer night sky like a stellar shotgun blast of lucid glitter, and the chorus of a family of singing crickets, are a great after dinner accompaniment.

I love to camp. I was raised hiking and camping almost every weekend.

We went on summer camps, winter camps, in between camps.

There were birthday surprise parties, and family reunions. There were Boy Scout summer camps, and hasty post-high school camps with friends who sneaked out of town with me.

The first times I tried to cook bacon and eggs in a paper lunch sack, my beagle ate well.

Camping has led to many family traditions. Family traditions have led to many camps.

I love to be outside, and I love to cook and eat well. I have spent a lot of time doing each. I've cooked professionally, eaten too much, and camped never enough. And somewhere along the way, I started doing all of these together. I'm not sure which time it was – I suppose I could guess, but it's not important.

What is important is the memories that come from these times and that I can share these memories with others. It's also important that I can share some of the things that I've done, and some of the things that I've heard of and seen. It's important to promote what you believe in.

Take these recipes, or even an idea that came from one or two, and go outside. Perhaps take along someone you love to talk to, or be quiet with.

Take your lover or family, or child, or dog. Or just take a friend. Take them, and your idea or perception of mine, and enjoy yourselves. Or just go alone. Outside. It's really the best place to be.

WELCOME

The rain had been coming down since about 9:00 in the morning. We had been in our canoes since 8:00. The river held its beauty in the rain. The sky was dreary and the smooth, flat water that had yesterday been so inviting, looked cooled by the rain. The steel blue sky showed no sign of clearing.

We canoed through the day, stopping for periods when the rain changed to lightning and thunder. We made our nights camp by about 4:00 and proceeded to set up and get out of the pervasive rain as soon as possible.

Potential tent spots were examined with scrutiny. Clotheslines sprang up under trees in relative dryness. A lean-to was quickly constructed over the picnic table we felt lucky to have. We gathered damp firewood before it got dark, just in case it cleared later. Canoes were beached, flipped over, and secured. Coolers were stashed within reach of the slowly drying table.

A slug of whiskey with a splash of water was given to each of us, those who smoked pulled out a cigar or cigarette from some well-hidden dry spot.

We looked around at the camp, up at the sky, at each other – then took a drink. Under the wrong conditions, this had all the earmarks of a really bad night. A bad night it was not.

That night, by lantern and candlelight, we enjoyed hot, home-made chicken noodle soup that had been warmed over the small cook-fire. Then we each had a small Caesar salad, stuffed mushroom caps, garlic/cheddar skin-on mashed potatoes, and perfectly seasoned, thick, juicy stuffed pork chops.

With stomachs full we sat there, slowly drying out under our tarp and talked by candlelight. It was a wonderful evening that I will never forget. Neither will any of my companions on that trip.

If you are a river rat like me, or a tent camper, you know of what I speak. It doesn't matter that it rained for 11 hours straight. You ended the day warm and dry – sipping on a cocktail, contented by your gloriously full stomach, with the fellowship of friends, and beautiful (albeit wet) surroundings. It cleared off later that night and the moon came out, seducing nearby coyotes into a beautiful mournful wail.

I believe that situations like these, like many times in life, are potentially steered by 'all the little things.' That's what counts for so much when you're camping.

Sometimes it makes the difference between just dry cereal for breakfast, or dry cereal with milk on top. (Nobody forgot the milk this time.)

Sometimes it means having that extra plastic bag over your new camera stowed in the bottom of the boat ("I didn't think we'd tip over, but we didn't see that rock until it was too late.")

Sometimes it means the difference between life and death. ("Nobody knew he had asthma, and his inhaler was at the bottom of his pack".) ("We forgot to bring a first-aid kit".)

I wrote this book to give readers an easy and enjoyable-to-read guide for cooking outside conventional means; away from microwaves, food processors, and digital timers.

Make no mistake – there is no need to sacrifice ease, taste, or food safety. There is no need for sacrifice. There is in fact, room for improvement upon convention.

It is often assumed that camp cooking has to be a sweaty, dirty, thankless job that yields luke-warm 'glop' served atop crisply scorched, dried out something.

I beg to differ. I beg to differ.

Oh, don't get me wrong – it's like that for many unfortunate people – but not for those who camp with me. And I want to share with you that making a gourmet meal is as easy out in the field as it can be at home.

Included in the book are also some various tips – from first aid to nature baths. I include these as additional bits of knowledge that I've learned over 25 years of camping, hiking, canoeing and kayaking, hunting, cooking, and more recently – guiding.

You can use these recipes anywhere – on the river, at deer camp, hiking in the mountains, or right at home sweet home.

The information is as accurate as possible, the memories as rich as text-laden paper will allow, and the stories mostly true. Some names have been changed to protect the guilty.

I sincerely hope you will enjoy reading it as much as I did learning, living and writing it.

Tony Kellar

"The clearest way into the universe
is through a forest wilderness"

~ John Muir ~

" I went to the woods to live, so
that I might live deliberately, and
learn what it had to teach me, so
that I would not, when it came time
to die, learn that I had not lived…"

~ Henry D. Thoreau ~

Following the path of least resistance is
what makes rivers and men crooked.

~ Anonymous ~

Camping
& Cooking

With the Bare Essentials

*Your Complete Guide to Easier Camping
and Gourmet Outdoor Cooking*

'Nature never deceives us; it is always
we who deceive ourselves.'

~Jean Jacques Rousseau~

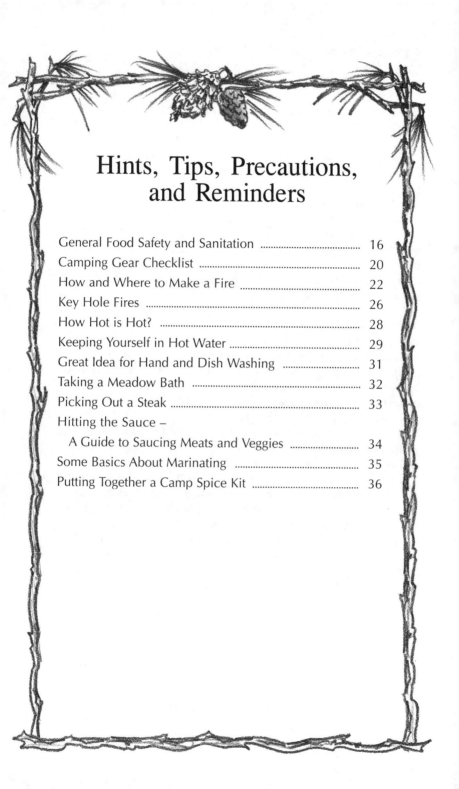

Hints, Tips, Precautions, and Reminders

GENERAL FOOD SAFETY AND SANITATION

Raw meats, like chicken, carry bacteria like Salmonella, which can cause illness, and in some cases, even death. Believe me, you don't want to run into food poisoning anywhere, let alone in the middle of nowhere.

Salmonella and most bacteria can be killed by heat. Chicken must be cooked thoroughly. When done, the meat should be opaque and the juices should run clear, not cloudy. Red meats like beef and venison can safely be eaten after being cooked less. Although ground meat is a higher risk, it too can be eaten while still almost red in the middle.

A common problem with food items like chicken (or any raw meats) is cross-contamination. Cross-contamination occurs when bacterium from raw or spoiled foods is transferred to other food via a common surface like cutting boards, knives, and hands.

This also could occur in a cooler that has raw meat that could leak juices into the ice water. Pull out a can of soda from that cooler and drink without washing it first, and you may as well head for the latrine right away. Take a good book.

This is one of the reasons raw meats should be double or triple wrapped in plastic, AND kept in a cooler with like items (items that will be cooked before consumption.)

A knife or cutting board that was used to prepare raw meat, if not thoroughly washed with HOT soapy water, will taint other foods. In fact, at home I keep a small spray bottle full of a diluted bleach solution that I spray utensils with after being washed, then wash them again. Counters and work areas get sprayed as well.

Additionally, it is commonly recommended that wooden cutting boards be used only for non-meat items. Wood is more permeable to bacteria and may not clean up as well as plastic cutting surfaces.

Treat all raw meat as if it is contaminated. Wash your utensils and hands well after handling. This goes for hand towels and aprons too. Hot soapy water must be used, and rinsed away well. The soap must be antibacterial in nature. Soaps like peppermint extract, though great for bathing outdoors will not suffice for sanitizing.

Meats cooked outdoors are especially delicious if cooked and handled properly. If not, the results can be awful! Ask anyone who has spent the evening on a camp shitter swatting mosquitoes, groaning, cursing and using up the weeks' supply of T.P. in one night.

Like I said before, the bacterium possible here can lead to serious illness requiring strong antibiotics or even medical care. Cook safely! To do so is really easy, it just requires a bit of extra attention, and perhaps a bit more time. When in doubt, err on the side of overcooking poultry!

As far as what temperatures are safe for what foods, keep these two numbers in mind: 140 and 40.

Those are your two gateway temperatures. Foods prone to bacteria growth should be kept at 40° or less for storage. Once heated, they need to stay at 140° to prevent the growth of dangerous bacteria. Any temperature above 40° and below 140° for more than a few minutes becomes a breeding ground for bacteria.

Exceptions to this are hermetically sealed containers like foil packets, cans, etc.

Danger foods or foods that are at especially high risk for bacteria growth include eggs, milk and meats. Anything with mayonnaise should be kept very cool, as it is one of the most dangerous. Even seemingly innocuous items like jelly and juice products will ferment if not kept cool.

When out in the field, it is often the traditional ice chest type cooler that is used to protect our food from dangerous temperatures, dirt, and pests. Though coolers are the best conventional method of food refrigeration when afield there are things that can be done to make the ice last longer and the cool air go farther.

• When loading coolers always allow room for plenty of ice. Block ice keeps longer than cubes or bags of cubes. Empty milk cartons and plastic pop bottles full of clean ice work as great fillers, and will melt to produce ice-cold drinking water.

• Be sure to keep iced beverages and the like in a separate cooler, away from cooled meats, cheeses, etc. Raw meat juice mixed in with the ice surrounding the beverages isn't good.

• Realize that the bottom of the cooler will stay the coolest, while the top of the inside will actually warm to dangerous temperatures occasionally, if exposed to very hot weather. Always put especially sensitive items like mayonnaise near the bottom and closest to the ice. Reserve the top area for less sensitive items.

• Keep the cooler out of direct sun if possible, and set it in a pool of cool water, a creek, or at least in the shade.

• The more the lid is taken off, the more warm air gets in and cool air gets out. You will substantially reduce the effectiveness of the cooler if you open the cooler a lot. Packing efficiently and chronologically will help to keep your cold food cold.

As an aid to food safety, I like to partially pre-cook chicken that I am taking on the trail. I grill it until it's just about half-way done. I then let it cool thoroughly. It takes less time to prepare at camp, and doesn't leak nasty raw juices all over.

Speaking of bears, if you are
in bear country, you may want
to forgo the citronella bug
spray. It has been said that some
bears are attracted
to the smell of citronella.
And it is easier after all to swat
mosquitoes than bears.

Table of Measurements and Conversions:

1 Tbs. = 3 tsp.
2 Tbs. = 1 oz.
1/4 cup = 4 Tbs.
1/3 cup = 5 1/3 tbs.
1/2 cup = 8 Tbs.
1 cup = 8 oz.
2 cups =1 pt.
1 qt. = 4 cups
1 gal. = 4 quarts
1 stick of butter = 1/4 lb. , or 1/2 cup,
   or 8 Tbs.
1 lb. loaf bread = about16-17 slices

I usually take a plastic lid, (like off of a can of vegetable oil spray) and see how much liquid it will hold. I then label it with a permanent magic marker (ie: 2/3 cup, etc) — this makes great double use of an item and saves on packing in a measuring cup or guessing.

CAMP GEAR CHECKLIST
TO MAKE THINGS EASIER

Clothing and Personal Gear:

- Pants, shorts according to weather – expected, and unexpected
- Shirts, short and/or long sleeves
- Socks, at least two extra pair
- Sneakers, boots or water shoes, and comfort shoes for camp
- Jacket or light coat
- Poncho or rain suit
- Swim suit and towel
- Bandanna. They have a million uses, and take no room to pack.
- Water bottle if desired
- Sunglasses

Personal Hygiene:

- Toothbrush and paste
- Floss
- Toilet paper, double wrapped in plastic
- Soap and shampoo – biodegradable
- Comb or brush
- Nail clippers

Safety and First Aid:

- First Aid kit – preferably professionally assembled
- Sunscreen
- Insect repellent
- Medications and allergy pills
- Eyeglass repair kit
- Signal mirror (polished aluminum)
- Needle and thread
- Superglue (also for emergency sutures)
- Whistle
- Fire starting kit

Shelter and Bedding:

- Tent and ground-cloth or tarp (carry a few extra tent stakes)
- Sleeping bag or fleece blanket
- Sleeping pad if desired
- Pillow if desired (option = extra clothes rolled up)

Hardware and Tools:

- Flashlight or head lamp, with extra bulb and batteries
- Waterproof matches and lighter
- Fire starting kit (tinder, kindling, see fire starting section of book)
- Pocket knife or multi-tool
- Small saw
- A few yards of strong twine or rope
- Duct tape

Community and Cook Gear:

- Plates and bowls
- Serving, cooking and eating utensils
- Mugs or drinking cups (no glass)
- Pots and pans as needed (plan out each meal)
- Can opener
- Stove and fuel if needed, or charcoal if needed
- Pot holder
- Coolers (see 'Tips on packing coolers')
- Water jugs
- Paper towels
- Aluminum foil
- Trash bags
- Dish soap, towels, and scrubbers

How and Where to Make a Fire

Certainly, the center of any camp is the fire. Be it in a remote, chilly northern campsite, or a rustic cabin in the mountains, a campfire really does warm more than your body.

Aside from the practical need for light and heat, the equally important part of a campfire or roaring fireplace gives us solace and warms our souls. That first whiff of camp smoke each year is truly good medicine for the soul.

Lighting a fire, and keeping it lit to meet your needs, isn't always as easy as you would hope. And the time spent waiting for heat, when one is truly cold, seems to take forever.

A fire needs three things: fuel, air, and a catalyst to start the process. Actually, air is part of the fuel needed, so that leaves you needing carbon fuel, and a catalyst.

A good cookfire can be gas, wood, or charcoal. The majority of my outdoors cooking utilizes wood.

Though I have used **gas (ie: propane)**, I generally don't prefer it. It has its benefits because it is clean, affordable, and reliable. I may use it for heating dishwater, or coffee – but not for grilling. For my tastes, it just doesn't lend that romantic quality of smoke, and cozy light. However, on rivers and in campsites that see frequent use, I encourage the use of gas and charcoal, as it will ease the pressure on the environment to provide firewood.

And though I have also used **charcoal** – I certainly prefer wood. There is a tendency to end up with the taste of chemicals in the food, and charcoal just isn't the warm friendly presence that a campfire is. *However*, the use of briquettes while using **Dutch Ovens** is certainly preferred over wood coals. Their heat and longevity are quite even and predictable – a necessity with Dutch Ovens!

I tend to get a little particular about my campfires. They are the beacon that every camp needs to warm, welcome, serve and protect.

I like to have a big fire at night as much as anyone, but it's important to make sure one is being **ecologically aware when collecting wood and starting fires.**

The guide service that I work for solves this problem by cutting their own firewood from woodlots that are being cleared, etc. – and transports it to our base camps which have semi-permanent fire pits. This solves the dilemma for us.

Many parks have guidelines or even rules set into place, to protect the woods from being depleted due to overzealous campers and hikers.

There are many rivers that have rules prohibiting open fires without a fire-pan. A fire-pan is simply a metal pan a few inches deep and 20 or so inches across. This prevents not only raging bonfires, but also protects the ground from unsightly fire-pits scattered all over.

And for Gob's sake, if you need an aid in collecting wood, and getting it to the desirable size ... use a saw!

Unless necessity dictates, or you are PROFICIENT with an axe – leave that to Mr. Bunyan. A quality wood saw is more than enough, and hatchets and axes are too often swung around by some idiot who 'saw someone do it on TV one time.'

Besides, anyone with any experience in the matter can tell you it is the saw that is often the easier and faster tool, let alone safer in the hands of a novice. Gashing open a shin, forehead or hand is never macho and can be just a bit dangerous, especially out in the wild.

Pick out a good **tree saw** meant for camping, or a small, aluminum, half-circle type that's sold for limbing trees and cutting small logs. Use the saw to get the wood into appropriate sized pieces for the fire, and stack it neatly.

Begin with a flat, dry place to start your fire. It should have a light breeze, and not subject to gusty winds. Take into consideration the presence of tents, lean-tos, and overhanging tree branches when placing the fire, and accept the fact that the wind may change directions, taking the smoke with it. You'll have to deal with it.

Also, if a fire has been made somewhere before, use that established spot. I've seen otherwise seemingly intelligent people march into the woods, and demand to make a fire where it suits them and not what would appeal to common sense.

Remember, no matter what the length of your stay – you are a temporary visitor here and nature should be impacted as little as possible.

Compile a small bunch of dry twigs, the smallest in circumference that you can find. Look to other, larger pieces for offshoots that may be broken off. Often around the bases of trees or deadfalls is a good place. These twigs should be no thicker than a wooden match. A bit of paper, dry grass or leaves, shaved bark, or dry pine needles make a good lighting aid. (Tinder)

In an **emergency (not just a hurry – an emergency)** look for a low hanging birds nest. They are usually made of dry, fine materials.

You will also want a larger pile of thicker wood. Go for the ones about as thick as a drinking straw, and work up. An easy fire to light is one that utilizes progressively larger wood. The most common errors are either beginning with wood that is too big, or not having enough kindling to catch and light the larger sticks.

A common and effective way to set up the fire is tipi style, with the smallest twigs in a pile sitting atop a few short pieces of slightly larger wood, then lean slightly bigger sticks together. This way the fire gets air from underneath when it needs air most … when trying to be born.

Also the fire will burn not only up, but down, creating that essential bed of coals ASAP.

If there is a strong wind or gusts that may threaten blowing out the first few delicate flames, make a quick wind block with your larger wood, a backpack, or other suitable items. Though, if this is the case, you may be wise in reconsidering a fire there to begin with.

There are a few simple rules: (1) Build your fire progressively. Start with the smallest wood, and work up. (2) Make sure you have enough tinder and kindling, to go all the way, before even lighting a match. It's real hard to keep one stick burning alone. (3) Make sure you have more than enough to make it through the evening, before it gets dark. Romping around the woods in the dark is a great way to break a leg. (4) In state parks and private camps it's always nice to come to a campsite that has been left clean, and with a bit of spare firewood which you can use. Use it. Give it back to those who will follow. (5) Don't go burning a bunch of trash in the fire before someone is going to cook on it. This also seems common sense, but you'd be surprised.

Never put plastic, styrosatanfoam, or glass or foil into a fire. These items are meant to be carried out. Anything left behind should wash away and return to the earth naturally in the next good rain, not the next millennium.

When starting a fire, I haven't always been blessed with perfect, dry kindling. This, actually, is often the case. There are a few neat **tricks** to circumvent this problem.

• Pack in commercially made fire-starters. They can also be homemade versions. Generally, just shredded paper and sawdust in a thin coat of paraffin wax. Or a cotton-ball rubbed with petroleum jelly. The commercially made fire starters come in several varieties and are dirt cheap, light, clean and easy to use.

• An old Boy Scout trick was to keep a couple stubs of thin tapered candles in our pack. The butt end of an old **candle**, when lit and placed under a pile of wet kindling, will dry out the sticks and light a fire as it goes.

• Dryer lint makes great tinder, to touch off the rest of your kindling.

• Take a dry stick, as big around as your thumb, and whittle the end of it, but not all the way to the end. The stick should have a 'beard' of dry shavings, 1-2 inches long. A few of these will aid in starting your fire.

However you choose to start your fire, make dang sure it's out before leaving it. Generous amounts of water should be poured on, then stirred into the coals. That fire can live for a long time, if you don't put it out all the way to the coals.

The entire pit, as well as each log and coal should be cool to the touch before you decide it's okay to leave.

Every year tens of thousands of acres of pristine forest are destroyed because of some **moron** who thought he could leave the coals to burn themselves out. These woods aren't just ours. They are the habitat for multitudes of animals and plants, many which are already clinging for dear life. A careless camper can mean the destruction of infinite acres of habitat.

This leads me right into another related topic. " L.N.T." These are three very important initials. They stand for **leave no trace**. This means everything from using given fire pits, to the conservative manner in which you should collect firewood, to where you should take a **forest dump**. You can have a nice warm fire, but don't leave any sign of where the wood came from. Don't leave ashes scattered about. Don't leave anything scattered about except leaves and shadows.

Don't leave garbage, no matter how small or biodegradable behind. Don't go tromping through virgin brush if there's a trail.

Don't cut down *any* trees for wood. Use the stuff that's 'dead and down'.

In general, remember that you are only a temporary user of these resources. We all have to share the space that we are allotted as do the other animals and plants. They were here first and will be here when we are gone. Enjoy the woods. Enjoy the solitude, and quiet peace. And leave the same, undisturbed woods for others.

KEY-HOLE FIRES

When cooking in an established pit, such as your lodge or backyard, this is a great multi purpose design for your fire pit.

Picture the traditional round design for a fire pit – imagine a circle. Now, remove a rock or two at "6:00".

Using additional rocks, run two parallel rows of rocks out from the hole, making an 'arm' that comes away from the fire a foot and a half, or so. The inside of this 'arm' should be hollow 10 inches or so. The pit, if viewed from above, should resemble an old fashioned keyhole. Due to prevailing north winds, put this 'arm' out from the fire ring to the north.

For a permanent fire-pit I highly suggest digging the earth out of the pit, down about 6-10 inches, including the 'keyhole.'

Functionally, this allows you to do several things, not as easily done with a round fire, especially a fire which is meant to cook, provide light, and surrounding warmth at the same time.

The fire pits surface area can be split up to do certain things in different areas.

1. Make main fire in large area. Scoop, or pull coals into 'arm' as needed, for cooking. Lay skillets, grills and such across rocks on 'arm' spanning the coals underneath.

2. You may now cook at the desired heat, and still have a nice hot fire (at the round end, away from the 'arm'), to keep you warm. This also provides a steady supply of new coals to maintain cooking temperature. If the weather is warmer, it allows you

to tend to your cooking directly, without suffering from the intense heat of the main fire.

I try to dig in my 'arms' on the north side of the fire, so as to allow me to avoid the smoke from the main fire, while cooking. I hate it when I feel more smoked than the food I am preparing.

Also with a good northerly breeze, this is a great place to light your initial fire. Your kindling pile will be somewhat shielded from gusts that may blow a struggling fire out, yet able to take advantage of the wind through the keyhole.

The wind blowing down and through the tunnel will also keep the mature fire and coals burning hot.

JUST HOW HOT IS 'HOT' ?

How and where to find the temperature dial on a campfire:
At home, in a conventional cooking arena, telling the temperature of the stove is a quick trick. But for many outdoor cooks, this area is not much more than guesswork. And without a thermometer it will remain so. But because this isn't always convenient or possible, here are some pointers.

Being at least somewhat accurate is necessary, because different foods will need different amounts of both time and heat to cook properly.

A thin chicken breast cooked over a raging hot heat for a half-hour, well ... it would be charred, tough, and juiceless. Nasty.

At the same time, a pork roast cooked uncovered over medium heat for a half-hour is raw.

The right approach to the heat begins with a simple gauge of the temperature at the foods cooking level.

Many cooks use the 'hot hand' method. Holding your hand over the grill, at cooking level, will tell you about how hot it is there.

Carefully place your hand, palm down, over the grill, as close to the grill surface as possible. (Without touching – duh.) Leave your hand there, and count seconds until your palm reaches the point of feeling very hot, just before uncomfortable. For example:

HOT FIRE = 2 second count = about 400°-450°
  Coals will appear orange, with little ash present.

MEDIUM FIRE = 4 second count = 350°-375°.
  Coals glow through a thin layer of
  "gray flannel" ash.

LOW FIRE = 5-6 second count = 300°-350°.
  Coals are wrapped in a thick layer of
  "gray flannel" ash

VERY LOW (or slow) FIRE = more than 7 seconds
  = less than 300°.

Little or no glow is visible, but heat is detected. This is the target temperature for smoking and some slow barbecuing.

Always be aware of the time and temperature required to cook food correctly. Be aware that campfires and coals will provide a dependable heat source, but one that may vary. Keep a watchful eye on this.

*See also the section on cast-iron and Dutch Oven cookery for further details on fire and coal temperatures.

KEEPING YOURSELF IN HOT WATER:

Hot water is an important staple to have at camp. It is needed in so many things. I don't care if you can tolerate your coffee luke-warm, and have the stones to bathe in ice cold stream water – you still need hot water. Dish and hygiene needs dictate that the water must be hot!

So, how do we do it? The best method for larger, more **semi-permanent camps**, is what I call the coffee pot method. And it has nothing to do with heating the water in a coffee pot.

Begin with an aluminum can, say about 4-5 gallons in capacity. This will depend on your access to clean water, and your need for hot water. Just keep reading, you'll get it.

Perhaps the best style would be one square in shape, if you can get it. Otherwise, you'll have to use rocks placed alongside the can to keep it from rolling. Here we go.

Lay the can on its side. The pour-spout, originally on top, should now be on one side. Roll, or adjust the can, so the hole is as far from the ground as possible, yet the can is still flat on its side.

On the side that faces up, poke a hole about the size of a nickel in the can, far towards the 'back', originally the bottom. Insert a funnel into this hole. Place the can (on its side) on a hot surface, on rocks over coals for example. If you are using a round can, you will have to secure it so it won't roll.

Pour water into funnel, until water almost comes out the spout. Let the water heat. Then, when hot water is needed, figure out how much you need, and add a like amount to the funnel. The water will then overflow out the spout, hot.

The principle here is **displacement**. If you fill the can to the level of the spout, heat the water, and then add 2 quarts cold water through the funnel, about two quarts of hot water will overflow out the spout.

For smaller quantities, more suitable to everyday camping, see the next page.' I've got a sweet little set-up that will solve your hot water needs perfectly.

GREAT IDEA FOR HAND AND DISH WASHING

This is the all-time most convenient, no-hassle way, for dispensing hot water. I won't take credit for its invention, but I will say that many happy campers have seen me use it and have made their own rigs.

I take a bucket full of hot clean water and a large plastic coffee-type mug, with a handle on it. The handle has had the bottom cut away, so that it slips over the edge of the bucket and hangs. It also has a hole drilled through near the bottom. I dip it in the hot water to fill it, then hang it on the bucket. Water slowly pours out the hole, under which I hold my hands, dishes, utensils, etc. for washing.

TAKING A MEADOW BATH

Sure, you can just scrub down a bit with a wet rag and call it a bath, but there are ways to really enjoy a more rewarding wash in the great outdoors.

This is a modification of the way a buddy of mine has his outdoor shower set up at his cabin. He uses a barrel that has about a 45-gallon capacity that is up on a 4x4 platform. He attached an old spout off a watering can and a pull chain.

The barrel is painted black on the outside, and is filled with rainwater that is collected from his gutters. The top of the barrel has two layers of screen folded over the top, to keep out bugs, and pine needles, and the like.

The collected water sits and is warmed by the sun. It's simply amazing how fast the water heats up!

I mean, this is no Hilton, but it does make nice warm shower water. You just stand under and pull the chain and are rinsed in nice, soft warm water. There's really nothing like it. (The water runs off into a trough that goes to his flower and veggie garden.)

To make use of the same principal in camp we just use extra-sturdy black trash bags.

Lay them on a flat spot, or even in a slight depression and carry water in from the river, or lake in a can or bucket. The bags will only hold 5-7 gallons each, tied shut. Using two bags (one for wash, one for rinse) is the way to go.

Let them lie in the mid-day sun for 3-4 hours at least. The sun's warmth will collect in the water, and if you carefully untie the bag, and sit down in it, it does provide tepid-to-warm water.

Like I said, it's no claw-foot hot-tub, but it's a lot better than having to expel the primal scream that always looses itself when taking a dip in springs icy cold waters.

If you are with someone you can trade favors with, maybe they'd be kind enough to add a bit of hot water from the campfire, when asked.

WHEN PICKING OUT A STEAK

You will surely want the most tender, flavorful cut that is available. Sometimes, due to cost, or market selection, this may not be possible.

I have listed what I believe to be the best cuts of **beef** for steak, down to the least tender cuts. If you pick from cuts near the bottom of the list, you may want to consider marinating them overnight to tenderize them. This will turn some of the toughest pieces into more tender ones, due to the breakdown of the muscle tissue by the acids in the marinade. Pick either store-bought marinade or make your own at a fraction of the cost.
(see also, MARINATING)

Most tender	1. TENDERLOIN - (FILLET MIGNON)
	2. CHUCK TOP BLADE
	3. TOP LOIN
	4. PORTERHOUSE/T-BONE
	5. RIB EYE
	6. RIB
	7. CHUCK EYE
	8. TOP SIRLOIN
Least tender	9. ROUND TIP

Sometimes, it will work to your advantage to purchase the 'lesser' steak. For example, you probably don't need to buy beef tenderloin to make up a batch of Fajitas. The recipe calls for a strong, thorough marinating, time that will tenderize a lesser cut of meat to sublime perfection. A more cost-effective way would be to go the route of round tip steak, or some chuck. By the time it sits in marinade for 4 hours or more, it will have a lot of tenderness added.

My uncle Ed generally buys chuck roast on sale and grills it like thick steak – it's beyond belief! With a little garlic, salt and pepper, it's the best $2.00 steak ever!

HITTING THE SAUCE WHILE GRILLING AND SMOKING: SAUCES, MARINADES, AND RUBS

You may want to avoid application of sauces too early in the cooking stage, unless you are going for a specific finished texture. Generally, wait till the last 10-20 minutes or so, to brush on any sauce. This avoids the sauce getting overheated, and charring.

Any sauces that contain tomatoes, jam, honey, molasses, or a lot of sugar and/or spice are more prone to scorching.

Meat may regularly be brushed with a marinade that is wine, beer, or water based, as this will evaporate, or soak in, for the most part. It is the thicker sauces that you will want to reserve.

Keep in mind that any marinade that has had raw meat in it, is potentially contaminated with bacteria that comes from the meat. Before this should be applied to any meat that is cooking or cooked, bring it to a rolling boil in a saucepan for at least 3 minutes, while stirring. It should then be safe to use again, as a baste on the cooked meat.

To marinate meat generally means to soak it in a liquid that will not only impart its flavor to the meat, but will also **tenderize** it.

The ingredients of the marinade may vary immensely, but most of them have one thing in common. That is the fact that they will contain some form of acid, often citric acid. Others may include vinegars or wine, or other alcohol. While the meat soaks and absorbs the marinade, the acid will begin to break down the muscle tissue, making it tender.

Most red meat will be best if marinated for no less than 3 hours, often overnight. This will depend on 3 things:

- The amount of flavor desired from marinating.
- The tenderness of the meat prior to marinating.
- The natural mildness of the meat (i.e.: fish won't soak as long before losing it's own flavor, and tasting just like the marinade.)
- Lighter meats like fish, chicken, and even pork need much less time to marinate. Think more along the lines of 1 hour. Delicate fish like tuna steaks won't need more than 1/2 hour.

BASIC MARINADE FOR BEEF, PORK, AND WILD GAME

    2   cups red, white, or blush wine
        A splash of Worcestershire sauce, or teriyaki
        A splash of Italian dressing
  1/2   Tbs. granulated garlic
  1/2   Tbs. ground black pepper

This is about as simple as it gets. Beer is often substituted for wine, or in addition to the wine. You may wish to add chili powder, or soy sauce. You can really make up your own recipe, keeping in mind the two most basic ingredients: acid and flavor.

Try to keep the marinade very 'watery' though, as opposed to 'thick'. The less that sticks to the outside of the meat during grilling, the better. For example, if you wanted a real chili taste, marinate well, then add a chili paste at the end of grilling. Otherwise, thick powders, and pastes will scorch during the grilling process, distorting and sometimes ruining the desired taste.

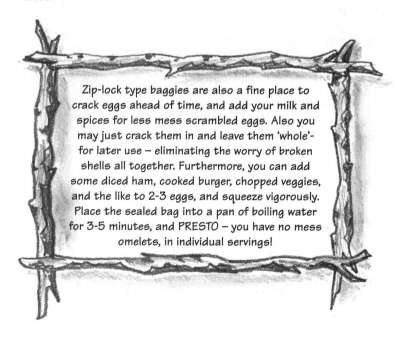

Zip-lock type baggies are also a fine place to crack eggs ahead of time, and add your milk and spices for less mess scrambled eggs. Also you may just crack them in and leave them 'whole'- for later use – eliminating the worry of broken shells all together. Furthermore, you can add some diced ham, cooked burger, chopped veggies, and the like to 2-3 eggs, and squeeze vigorously. Place the sealed bag into a pan of boiling water for 3-5 minutes, and PRESTO – you have no mess omelets, in individual servings!

PUTTING TOGETHER A SPICE KIT:

Every camp should have a few good kits. A good first aid kit is the most important.

Having a little bag of tricks stashed away has been the secret to success for many professions and hobbies. This little bag of tricks will help to enrich any outdoor menu item, and takes up little room.

If you have a particular recipe with a long list of dry spices and herbs, this may be a good place to start. If they are all dry, and they will be mixed together at the same point in a given recipe, you may as well do it ahead of time.

Measure out specified amounts, and combine in a baggie, or small container. Be sure to label the bag, and pack it away.

There's no use in packing in dozens of spice containers if they are only to be used once or twice. Additionally, think about the spices you'll want for the whole trip.

Some outdoor stores sell little 'multi-spice' containers. They hold a bit of 6 or 7 spices apiece and are ingenious.

In general, I would suggest the following as the basics for any camp box.

1. Salt and pepper
2. Garlic powder
3. Cayenne or other hot pepper powder
4. Onion flakes
5. Basil/Oregano blend
6. Bouillon cubes – a few chicken flavored, a few beef.
7. Sugar or honey

Keep in mind that the spices will need to be protected from moisture.

• The single serving packets given away at fast food restaurants work great for a backpack or camp-box. Look for salt and pepper packets, dried hot peppers, mustard, mayonnaise, ketchup, soy sauce, pickle relish, etc. Mayonnaise is especially great as you can use it for sandwiches, etc. without opening a whole jar that would need refrigeration.

Many pizza makers now deliver little sealed cups of garlic butter, ranch dressing, and marinara. These don't need to be kept cool, and are quite easy to store.

A few notes about the items you will use for preparing recipes. Whenever possible choose the freshest ingredients. This may not always be possible, or desirable, considering cost, availability, ease, and the fact that some of the best outdoor and camp cookery happens on the spur of the moment, and you may find yourself ' just working with what you've got.'

As a sidebar, I'll briefly discuss herbs and spices. First of all, what's the difference between herbs and spices?

Herbs are generally the leaves and shrubbery of said plant. Spices are usually the other aromatic qualities of the plant. Parts like the berries, bark, buds and so forth.

For example, peppercorns are the berries of the plant in varying colors. The green ones are green at mid-life, they turn red, and then black, or brown as they mature. The only real functional difference is the color.

In some fancier dishes, say a complex white sauce; the chef may not desire the creamy white appearance of the sauce tainted with black pepper. The taste of white pepper is essentially the same. (Really, the only pepper that I actually recommend avoiding is that found on many sunny windowsills, in late summer – fly pepper.)

Cinnamon is another good example. The dried, peeled bark of the branches of the cinnamon plant is aromatic and imparts wonderful flavor.

The best rule of thumb when picking herbs and spices is this – the more aromatic the better. Those that have been on the shelf for a long period will not have the robust quality of their fresher counterparts. If using less fresh spices and herbs proves to be your only option, you may attempt to rejuvenate them a tad bit by lightly heating them in a hot skillet for a minute.

Just don't scorch them – burnt spices don't taste any better than stale ones.

"The wildlife of today is not ours
to dispose of as we please. We have
it in trust, and must account for it to
those who come after."

~King George IV~

Alternative
Cooking Methods

While away from home, you will find that nature will provide you with the opportunity to experiment with different approaches to food preparation.

Here are some ideas to try that may help some of those situations go smoother.

Campfire Grilling

PLEASE – I have seen so many new cooks make this mistake – I had to mention this: when grilling, resist the urge to press down hard on the meat with the spatula. Some people mistakenly think that this will speed up the cooking and won't hurt the food.

What happens is all the juices run out onto the coals, giving you a dry, juiceless, tough, scorched piece of meat suitable in my opinion only for resoling a moccasin.

Rather than trying to rush something to doneness and sacrificing texture, taste, and overall satisfaction, give it time. Let it slowly progress. 'Everything in its time.'

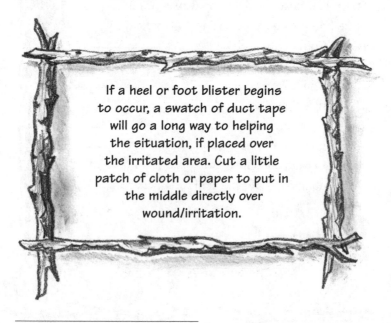

If a heel or foot blister begins to occur, a swatch of duct tape will go a long way to helping the situation, if placed over the irritated area. Cut a little patch of cloth or paper to put in the middle directly over wound/irritation.

Grilling Whole Fish

Butterfly the fish by cutting the entire length of the fish, through the ribs along the spine. Be careful *not* to cut too far through the skin, thus cutting fish into two pieces. Lay on a medium grill, skin side down, perhaps on a bed of greens. These could be whatever is handy.

Parsley or dill would be great, as would wild grape leaves, or even green grass. (Never use unfamiliar plants for cooking until you can determine that they are safe.) Lay on a thick coat of herb butter and a few lemon slices. Cook to desired doneness/ firmness. Depending on the thickness of the fish, you may wish to flip it over, to finish cooking through.

HELPFUL HINT: When thawing frozen fish, some claim that thawing it in cold milk, will help dispel frozen taste, and fish will taste "fresher".

USEFUL TIP: When cleaning fish, a few leftover bottle caps nailed to your cleaning board help scrape off the scales. Bottle caps are usually abundant around most fish camps. If not, it isn't really a fish camp.

USEFUL TIP: Fish is wonderful grilled, with the lightly smoky flavor of a few tea bags soaked in water, then laid on the hot coals. This produces a great, delicate smoky essence perfect for fish or shrimp.

Fish Sticks

Yes, it's a bad play on words, but a great method for cooking fish (or lots of other stuff for that matter).

Harvest a suitable length roasting stick, about as long as one you'd use for hot dogs. (In fact, save your stick to be used again.) Pick a stick that has a fork at one end. Leave the 'tines' of the fork at least as long as the fish or food that you will cook.

Wrap a piece of foil over the 'fork' a few times, across the space between tines, thus creating a nice foil surface for your food. Add food and cook. You could now, if desired, wrap another layer of foil around the food, tightly to steam it. Lay on some fresh herbs, or onions before wrapping.

The same method could be used similarly, bending a piece of wire coat hanger into a hoop, or square, and then proceeding with the foil. This way may be preferable to those who try to be super low impact. Hats off to them.

Please remember that tin foil is amongst the worst things that can be left behind, and takes decades to decompose. *If you bring it in, PACK IT OUT. That goes for all litter. Remember, kids learn most by watching adults – teach them well. Thanks.*

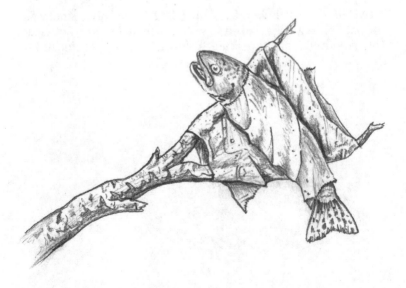

Boiling Water in a Paper Cup

Water and other liquid can be heated in a paper cup, and milk heated right in its paper/cardboard container, as long as it isn't waxed.

The fact that there is liquid on the other side of the paper keeps the paper from reaching its flashpoint.

Just set the cup or carton directly on hot coals.

Bear in mind that if the container is not full, the portion above the water line will eventually char and burn.

This comes in handy also for hard or soft boiling eggs on the trail.

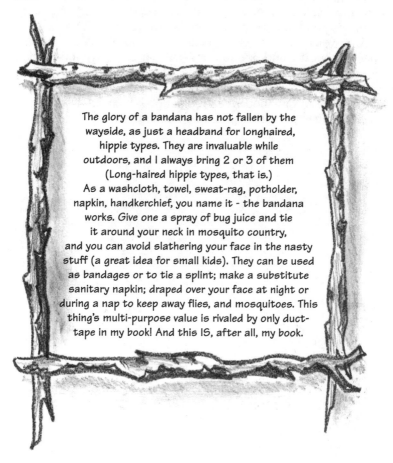

The glory of a bandana has not fallen by the wayside, as just a headband for longhaired, hippie types. They are invaluable while outdoors, and I always bring 2 or 3 of them (Long-haired hippie types, that is.)

As a washcloth, towel, sweat-rag, potholder, napkin, handkerchief, you name it - the bandana works. Give one a spray of bug juice and tie it around your neck in mosquito country, and you can avoid slathering your face in the nasty stuff (a great idea for small kids). They can be used as bandages or to tie a splint; make a substitute sanitary napkin; draped over your face at night or during a nap to keep away flies, and mosquitoes. This thing's multi-purpose value is rivaled by only duct-tape in my book! And this IS, after all, my book.

Bread on a Branch

Either roll the dough flat, to 1/4-inch thickness (you could use a flour-coated coffee can, or a bottle as a roller) or pull it into strips 6-8 inches long. Using a branch several feet long (wienie stick length), wrap the dough, ropelike, around the end of the stick. Or you could roll a piece into a ball, the size of a small apple, and stick it on the end of the stick.

Hold the dough stick over medium high heat, turning occasionally, to cook evenly, until the dough has risen, and is approaching golden brown.

Filling the cavity created by removing it from the stick, with butter and peanut butter, or jelly makes a great dessert. Although, removing it in one piece has been known to be a bit tricky.

This would be a rather impractical method of baking for many people, but it's kind of a fun project, that certainly works well, if you are caught without other means of baking. Hey … how wrong can it go?

Kids love this method when the dough is mixed with some cinnamon sugar and raisins prior to wrapping.

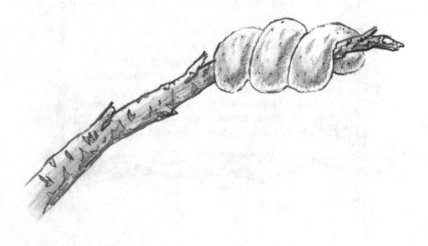

Tin Foil Dinners

The only things that make frozen 'TV dinners' as bad as they are, are the tasteless, bland ingredients and lack of imagination; foil dinners are a primitive way to make an easy meal, and make it well.

Granted, some of the more basic recipes are not that exciting, or that far from the TV-style dinner, and tend to be relegated to the Scout-o-Ramas. With just a bit of imagination, you or your scout can eat well with this method and be the envy of the rest.

This is the first way I was taught to cook dinner in Boy Scouts. As a younger scout on an overnight trip, I brought my first foil dinner, dads old sleeping bag, my pillow, and moms old duffel bag from college. Lots about camping have changed for me since then, but this is still a fail-safe way to cook dinner.

Traditional Foil Dinner:

Tear a large swath of foil from the roll – it helps to use higher quality foil. Place it shiny side up, on a clean work surface. In the middle of the foil, place a potato or two that have been thinly sliced (1/4"). Spread out the slices so they are overlapping, but not stacked up. On the potato, lay a hamburger patty that is seasoned the way you like. Over the patty, lay onion slices, in the same manner as before. Add carrot slices, or kernel corn, or whatever sounds good. Fold the foil over neatly, to completely cover the food. The foil should be folded in straight lines, and then "cuff" each fold. Wrap this in another piece of foil, the same way. You want to retain as much steam during cooking as possible. Lay this on a hot bed of coals for 10 minutes or so, then flip it over, to cook on the other side. After an additional 15 minutes or so, unwrap and eat.

Diamond Jim's Namekogan Chicken Dinner

My Dad took his turn at camp cooking a few years ago. Since his reputation for less than stellar cooking ability preceded him, we all secretly prepared by stashing extra jerky and trail mix that day.

Well, Dad got us good! He pulled out these pre-packed foil dinners and cooked them up and served them. They were extraordinary though simple.

Dad's directions went like this:

"I took some frozen boneless/skinless chicken breasts and thawed them and pre-cooked them. When they were done, I cut them into little pieces and mixed them with some dry onion soup mix. I scooped this onto pieces of foil, and added a little bit of bacon grease. Then I chopped up some baked potatoes and added this to the chicken."

Dad laid these on the grill and flipped them over after 10 minutes or so, then cooked them for another five minutes and took them off. He briefly opened each packet and laid on a piece of Swiss cheese, then quickly re-closed the foil.

Hey, look at the ingredients. How could this NOT be good?

Your options are unlimited for this type of cooking, and many a hungry hunter, Boy Scout, fisherman, and camper have eaten well, thanks to foil dinners.

Cooking in a Muffin Pan:

This method wouldn't be practical for many large meals or parties, but in the right situation, it works well. I first learned this in Boy Scouts and it worked well for us. It's another method that is so simple, it has to work. It is also convenient for backpacking and kayaking, as the pans take up little room and weigh almost nothing.

For four people, for example:

Get two 12-hole muffin pans, for full size muffins. Mix up some biscuit dough (see recipe). Ball up some burger mixed with bread crumbs, spiced to your taste. Each ball should be sized right to fill up a muffin hole about 1/2 to 3/4-way. Thinly slice up three potatoes, and a carrot, and perhaps a small onion.

Line four holes with muffin liners, and drop in four equal portions of dough. Spray four other holes with cooking spray, and put in veggie mix. In the last four holes, put the burger balls.

Lay the other pan UPSIDE DOWN, over the first. Clamp the pans together, either with a piece of wire, or whatever you come up with. On a small bed of coals, set down a few rocks, so their tops are just an inch or two above coal level. Lay the pans on the rocks, and shovel a light coat of coals over the top pan. Wait 15-20 minutes, and remove. There's dinner for four.

The simplicity of this method is only rivaled by its versatility. Just think of the breakfast options, or whatever you like. Enjoy.

You could adapt this method to use aluminum pie tins, or bread pans and have similar results, although the bread pan will work better if the bottom one is at least half full, and you may need to wrap them in foil, to prevent hot air escape.

St. Croix Cream Can Dinner

This is a recipe that I got from Rob, an old friend I met while canoeing the beautiful St. Croix River, dividing Minnesota and The Land Of Cheese.

We had camped for the afternoon and along came a couple of people, who ended up stopping, shooting the bull a bit, and sharing some of our beers. That's where I met Rob, who regularly canoes and camps with large groups. He said this is a tradition of theirs at their final landing, the last night.

I've tried it many ways and can attest it is one of the best ways ever of cooking for many people.

You will need an old-fashioned cream can – 7 to 10-gallon capacity, with the screw type lid. NOTE: I've been told that you need to use a can with welded seams, not soldered, or the solder will leach into the food. I solved the problem altogether by finding a used 'new style' milk can at an auction. It's stainless steel, holds about 4 gallons, and works GREAT!!

1	dozen ears of sweet corn, husked, and silk removed
10	lbs. potatoes, washed
2	lbs. carrots, washed, and peeled
2-3	large onions, peeled, and halved
3-5	rings dinner sausage, kielbasa-style, or what suits you
2-3	Quarts of water.

Optional: 1 can of dark beer (that's to cook with. Extra may be desired for the chefs consumption.)

Add potatoes and other veggies, including corn ears. Then add the sausages. Place a spare potato on top. Add beer, and water.

When you have a nice bed of coals, lay a grate, or poles over fire, to support can. Can should be within inches of coal surface.

Screw the lid on can LOOSELY so steam can escape. (Personally, I'd poke a hole or two in the top, as a relief valve. The steam *must* be able to escape!) You want the steam to stay in and cook the food, but it must be able to escape or you risk dangerous pressure inside can.

Place can over fire, a few inches above coals. If desired, you could throw a few coals on top of lid, to enhance heat.

Sit down in a comfortable spot, consume other beers as desired. Listen for boiling, and steam escaping (if none is, loosen lid a bit!). After an hour and a half of boiling, remove lid to see if top potato is done. When it is, chow down! You could pour contents into a clean, foil lined window planter for easier serving.

Serves, according to Rob, 10-15 hungry canoers, or 1 medium-sized black bear.

You could, of course, add other ingredients. A cut up chicken, near the bottom of the pile, or a handful of fresh herbs would be awesome. This could be modified, to include sea fish, or even game, such as rabbit. Just be careful to wash it properly, as no one likes fine hare in their dinner.

St. Croix Chicken and Shrimp

In the summer of 2003, while working as a guide for Missouri River Expeditions, I received a call from my boss saying that he had just booked a dinner for the local Kappa Alpha Theta sorority. Forty-five hungry college ladies would be critiquing my abilities!

I immediately thought of the milk can and went to work. It went wonderfully, and they loved it! I submit the following recipe with many thanks to those young ladies for the opportunity to cook for them. It was truly a pleasure.

In my stainless steel milk can, I put:

15	ears of corn, husked and silked, then cut in thirds
10	lbs potatoes, washed and trimmed
1/2	pound button mushrooms, fresh and sliced
3	green peppers, chopped
2	red peppers, chopped
1	small bag baby carrots, halved
3	large yellow onions, peeled and chopped
4	pounds frozen shrimp
1 1/2	dozen chicken legs
1 1/2	dozen chicken thighs
4	pounds loose Italian sausage
2	cloves elephant garlic- peeled, smashed and chopped
1	16 oz bottle of V-8 juice
1	bottle of Fat Tire premium dark beer
About 3	Tbs. Bay seasoning

This all filled the can to the absolute top! I put the lid on, and set the can atop 16 charcoal briquettes that were just hitting high temperature (glowing orange with little ash visible.) I had spaced out the charcoal so that they were evenly distributed under the can.

I set the steam release valve atop the can so that it was barely open, but checked it often until I saw steam coming out (for safety).

After 35 minutes I lifted the lid to find that the entire contents were cooked to perfection! Only 35 minutes! I had two large roasting pans at the ready, dumped the contents of the can into the pans, and garnished with fresh chopped chives and parsley.

The food was so tender and delicious! Being cooked in the steam had tenderized the meat to the point where it fell off the bone and all the juices had been locked in and not lost.The flavors had mingled together so well! The ladies loved it and were very thankful.

Naked on the Rocks –
Using Hot Rocks as a Cooking Surface

Don't expect to master this right away, but it is fun to experiment. The simpler the food to cook, the better it will go.

1. Find one or two appropriate sized rocks, flat. Allow them to warm gradually – don't heat them fast, as some will explode – a sure way to ruin any gathering. (Don't use flint, as it WILL explode) You may wish to spray them off with water, maybe a water/vinegar cleaning solution. *Do this while rock is still cool*, quickly cooling a hot rock may cause it to shatter.

2. Once hot, dust them off by blowing or wiping with green grass. (Use gloves!)

3. Go for it. Frying meat of almost any kind will go well here. Chicken breasts and burgers do well. Bacon is easy this way. Hot dogs are done in minutes.

Biscuits are also done well using this method. If you do need some oil, use peanut oil, as it stands higher temperatures. Just a touch will do. You may need to turn (rotate) the food occasionally. If you place an empty aluminum can, i.e.: coffee can, over the dough, then place a coal on top of the can, it will bake!

Eggs work great, if you have just the right rock. Perhaps laying a piece of foil on the rock will help? Warming up or toasting a bit of bread is a snap.

4. A great place to do your re-heating or slow warming. Just remember to monitor heat and turn food gradually to heat evenly.

Naked Corn on the Cob

Fresh sweet corn, enough, plus 5
Salt, pepper and spices
Bucket of water

Peel back husks, without removing from ear. Discard the silk, and place husks back in position. Soak the corn, whole, in enough water to cover corn. Water should be either warm or room temp. After 20 or so minutes, lay the corn on bed of coals, shaking off excess water. You may want to spread the coals out beforehand to accommodate a large batch of corn. Just make sure you still have a thick layer of hot coals under corn. Turn corn occasionally, blackening each side. When outside layer is thoroughly charred, remove one ear from fire for testing. Husks can be removed with a pair of heavy gloves. Dip in a jar of melted sweet cream butter, and enjoy. Be sure to have plenty of both napkins and toothpicks handy.

For feeding en' masse, I use wooden shish-kabob skewers as corn holders. Break them off about half way, and stick them in. At the end, they work as great toothpicks!

And this corn is really so good, you will never get away with just one or two ears per person! Prepare plenty of extras.

Making Your Own Rotisseries / Spits:
Chicken on a Twig

Serves Four – Generously

1 Amish roasting hen, whole
Spit stick
Medium fire – good hot coals

This is a classic recipe, perfect for those who are willing to put in a little extra work, accept a bit more of a culinary challenge, and take a few extra pats on the back.

You will need a green branch measuring about 1" in thickness. The branch should be stripped of its bark and any but the smallest protruding growth. Depending somewhat on the diameter of the fire, my sticks (spits) are usually about 3-4 feet in length.

This brings us to a good point. I encourage 'leave no trace' efforts, which would seem to contradict hacking down a perfectly good sapling.

Basically, yes. But stop to consider the true nature of the woods. (No pun intended.) By searching for twin saplings that are less than 4 feet apart, and removing one of them, you aren't hurting the forest growth. Actually, you are promoting strong growth, of the remaining tree.

See it this way. As young saplings, they are already competing for moisture, sun, and nutrients. As they grow to "teenage trees", their branches will be touching or already interfering with each other. As they continue to grow they will fight each other and neither will have the room it needs for optimum growth. Overcrowding is nature's way, to some degree (look at us, as a case in point).

To remove a sapling for use, and doing so in a conscious manner, is not a sin. Especially if you make it a habit to pick up others' litter, and follow other good conservation rules religiously. The surviving tree will have the space it needs to grow up stronger, and healthier. Left together, they wouldn't both survive. Cut the sapling as close to the ground as possible, to avoid leaving a point sticking out of the ground to be tripped over, or painfully stepped on.

You will also need two sticks with a 'y' shape at the top. These needn't be green, but they must all be sturdy. They will be used as end-posts on which to rest the center stick. They should be about as big around as your thumb, or a touch thicker. They should stand about 3 or 3 1/2 feet long.

After burying the one end ('y'-up) in the ground at least 8-12 inches, the 'y' must be (depending on the fire again) about 2 1/2 feet high. The goal here is to rest the long stick, in the crevices (Y) of the two other sticks and have it support the chicken, at a height suitable for roasting.

Generally, given a fire consisting mainly of a nice hot bed of coals, you will want about 1 1/2 feet of air below chicken. If needed, you may wish to poke a third green stub into the coals, high enough to help support the chicken, on the spit.

Slide chicken down the long, stripped pole, inserting the stick through the vent, (the rear end to some of you) and coming out the neck, or vice-versa. Bring chicken to about half-way, centered on the pole, and rest on 'y' poles. If, when skinning the spit pole, you can leave a protruding branch, at the bottom of one end, this can be propped up by another stick to hold the spit, in stages, as you turn it. Turn occasionally, so as to heat entire bird, to a sweat.

Then the second time around, it's lightly browned then the third – finished.

This is the critical part. The inside must cook thoroughly, before the skin is browned. The bird must cook slowly – don't try to rush it! I really recommend cooking this meal while you still have good light, so you can monitor cooking progress. If not, use a flashlight, or lantern.

When you think the bird is done, pick the inside of a thigh or breast, and make a small incision, to the bone. (See 'poultry cooking and handling tips'.) If juices run clear, and NOT PINK, it's time to serve. If you have a meat thermometer, the temp on the inside of a thigh, next to the bone should read 175°.

This is accompanied nicely by garlic mashed potatoes, baked beans, and a loaf of hot bread. It's a meal for one who is either quite adept at outdoor primitive cooking, or very sure of their ability to quickly become so. If done right, it's a most impressive meal, and one that your guests will surely tell others about enthusiastically!

This method, followed similarly, would work with just about anything you wished to spit, except watermelon seeds.

HINT: A pair or two of wooden skewers stuck through the bird, in an 'X', close around the spit, will help prevent the bird from spinning on its own, a semi-common difficulty. (*See illustration*)

The Dangle Spit

This is a great way to cook, works like a charm, and is centered on a simple principle. That is … a piece of thin rope or twine, when twisted, will unwind itself. And if weight is hung from it, it will 'over-unwind', and wind back the other way, in an effort to straighten out.

So, if one were to use a tripod, tree branch, or a strongly supported stick hung over a fire, and tie on a piece of braided twine or rope, and from this hang food to be roasted, they would have a somewhat self turning vertical spit!

A few tricks here are:

- Attach a small piece of light chain to the bottom (fire) end of the twine, this will make hooking the roast holder easier than tying it on.
- A small stick, stuck through the twine horizontally, will make a nice handle, with which to wind up the twine.
- The more twine, the longer the twisting, before it will stop, and need rewinding.

I've seen a similar approach work well. I camped with some folks in Montana who had a small (2-3 qt.) pot tied to a twine hanging from an overhead limb. The bottom of the pot passed just above the highest of the flames from their rather small fire.

As they only wanted to cook with slow, medium heat, they simply gave the pot a tiny push. It swung back and forth over the fire. Had they wanted to cook even slower, they'd have just swung it a little wider or higher, or both.

Another method of getting the dangle spit to turn itself: Flatten an aluminum foil pie tin, attach it fly-swatter style to a short stick, then attach stick to the twine or rope above the food being cooked. This will give you a fan hanging above the food. The hot air rushing up from the fire will push away the fan, causing the string or chain to twist. Also works well in breezes.

The Art of Pit Cooking

Ahh – the pit … so many wonderful memories. I have memories of doing this, or at least being around it, clear back to age ten or so. My parents were young camping and pic-nicking freaks. Today they're older and are just freaks.

I will always remember the first time I saw a pit cook. It was with them, along the Missouri River, on the Nebraska side near Gavins' Point Dam. It was a huge weekend soiree, and there had to be 15 or more people there. The food just kept coming, and coming, and coming. It was some of the best food I've ever had! I can remember it that clearly, yet I was no more than nine or ten years old!

It is a little labor-intensive and may not be for everyone or every occasion. But for those who want a real cooking adventure and challenge – this is it.

Anyway, the basic idea is this, follow these instructions even vaguely, and you will have an awesome meal! The juices and flavors are sealed in with the food, and the heat is constant. You could conceivably undercook some food, like chicken, but it would be hard to really *overcook* it. (When in doubt, give it an extra half-hour. Better over cooked, than under.)

This can be done in dirt or sand and it will work great.

You will need a good pair or two of heavy heat resistant gloves, maybe leather welder's gloves. Also a whisk broom, shovel, lots and lots of wood, and an afternoons time (most of which will devoted to relaxation and playtime rather than prep or cook time.)

Dig a pit about 4-5 feet across and 4-5 feet down. Throw in some rocks, from the size of an apple on up to the size of a muskmelon. Say 5-8 rocks total. Now build a good hot fire in the pit. Keep it burning. When you have coals that are a good 8-10 inches deep and still a good flame, lay some boards (NOT 'green treated') or logs as big around as your arm, across pit. On these lay more rocks, say another 10-15 or so. Then lay on more firewood. ⸕

At some time, the wood will burn through, and the rocks will drop, spreading over the heart of the coals. Now it's time to add your food.

Whole chickens or cut up turkeys work great (so as to fit in the pots). You could do roasts, fish, hams, pork roasts or chops, anything you want. Stuff a bunch of veggies in with the meat. Say you're doing a chicken or roast, throw in some sliced onions and carrots, and celery. Potatoes are awesome here! Try some mushrooms. Don't forget to stuff the cavity of the bird with veggies, or maybe halved apples.

Maybe you'll drape some raw bacon strips over the bird or roast. You could make a pan full of sliced acorn squash, de-seeded, with a dollop of brown sugar, and molasses, in each divot.

This is a great time to experiment. Feel free to try anything that you'd roast in the oven at home, being mindful that it must be totally sealable in it's pot or pan. Try lots of recipes that might interest you. You are only limited by the size of the pit you've dug.

Cook anything you want, but cook a lot! Make a huge batch of skin-on-roasted garlic mashed potatoes. Make sweet corn, roasted in its husk, or in a Dutch Oven. Make some of that green bean and bacon casserole stuff with the little crunchy onion things on top. Make scalloped corn with a breadcrumb crust. Make anything!

If you are using a Dutch Oven with a tight lid- that works awesome. Otherwise, you can use those blue speckled baking pans, or most any good pan with lids. Make sure each pan is sealed up extra-well with foil. (*need I say this? – no plastic handles!*) And wimpy, thin aluminum may warp.

Lay these pots in the fire pit, on the hot rocks/coals. Lay them so they are stable and won't tip over in the steps ahead.

I like to have a barrier between the pans and the dirt or sand above. I like to use a couple of pieces of foil to just lay on top of the pans. I've also seen people use a wet old canvas tarp. A layer of green grass or leaves would do in a pinch. You'll see why you'll want a barrier, in a minute.

Next, gently cover the pit with several inches of dirt or sand. I'd say you want at least a foot of cover over the pit. The whole thing, edges and all should be thoroughly covered with fill. This will trap in your heat and do your cooking for you.

After about 3 hours has passed, it's time to eat.

Put on your gloves again and grab the shovel. As you GENTLY dig down to the pots, you'll know when you are close, as you'll see the foil. This prevents you from accidentally digging too deep and knocking the lid off a pot, while covered with dust and coals.

Lift the foil aside, bring the pots out, and uncover. If you have compressed air handy (if you're at home) this works great for blowing the ashes off the lids before removal. Or substitute a quick whisk-broom.

Gather everyone around and let them get a whiff of the awesome smells that come rushing at you in the steam that floats away as you de-lid. Grab a plate, load up, and enjoy what will certainly be called a triumph of culinary achievement, underground. So tender, so juicy! I'm not kidding, meat cooked like this literally falls off the bone it's so tender! And juicy! Make sure your guests have plenty of napkins, because this stuff will be dripping with cooked-in natural juices and flavor! The vegetables will be delicious, steamed and bursting with co-mingled flavors.

Some people like to add some water to the coals, right before covering up the fire. This produces a lot of hot steam, but isn't necessary when using pots and Dutch Ovens. It works well when cooking without any pots, and instead wrapping your food in leaves, and grass. Wild grape leaves are great to wrap your food in to cook. Just be sure that there is enough greenery under the food to prevent burning, and enough over to keep out the dirt.

This is where you want to be extra careful, when digging back into the pit, at chow time. For food wrapping, also consider cornhusks, and other broad leaves, like cabbage, and lettuce.

Either way, but especially without pots, consider tossing on some fresh herbs before covering. The aromatic scent of rosemary, or dill gives food a great flavor. *Never ever use pine, cedar or other evergreen materials for smoke.*

Smoking Fish and Meat

I asked a friend of mine once if he'd ever smoked fish. His reply was "Yeah, I tried it once in college but I couldn't keep it lit."

Aside from smart remarks like this, smoking meats may be done on any grill, and to several degrees. Given a certain heat and longer time, it will dehydrate, and assume a jerky-like texture.

In this section, I'm going to be referring to the method used to simply add a wonderful essence to meats already being grilled. It's quite easy, and is a great twist that any beginner should feel comfortable trying. This is a perfect example of a method anyone can use. Try it perhaps one time, and judge the results for yourself! You will almost automatically, through the cooking experience, and tasting what you've created, see your own ways to fine-tune it. Then next time, maybe for a few guests, repeat the process with confidence and add your own touches. Here, you're on your way to gourmet.

The premise is this: you are grilling, but the coals are a bit deeper and not as hot, the grill a bit higher and the cook time longer. With the addition of some wet aromatic wood chips or sawdust – you're smoking!

Smoking uses indirect heat, rather than the direct heat given to burgers, etc. The heat is accumulated and held under a domed lid, and the food is baked in smoke more than grilled.

Aromatic woods that are famous for their bolder, smoky essences are those such as apple, hickory, pecan, plum, alder and mesquite. Don't use evergreen (i.e.: pine, cedar, fir) branches or wood for smoking. They give off a resiny thick smoke. I mean, it's fine for a campfire, but not to smoke food with. And this is one spot where less is more. A thick heavy cloud of white smoke will absolutely tarnish the taste.

Other items create a different subtle flavor of their own. Fresh herbs such as rosemary, thyme, and oregano will contribute their flavors. Wild grapevine trimmings are wonderful to smoke delicate meats. Even soaked teabags laid on the coals will lend a nice essence, delicate and perfect for fish and shrimp.

For best results, soak the smoking medium in very wet water for an hour or so prior to use. (Always avoid the pre-packaged dehydrated water sold in some bait stores.) Soaking will aid the chips or herbs in smoking rather than just burning up.

Lay the wood chips in a circle around the outside of the coals. In the center, set a tin pie pan, or other wide/shallow metal container. This will catch the drippings from the meat and prevent flare-ups. Place the meat directly over the drip pan. Water may be added to the drip pan, to provide some residual humidity while cooking.

The grill should be higher from the heat, than usual. The height really depends on the thickness of the meat. The meat should be cooked in a very smoky, hot 'oven'. Place the grill or smoker lid on tightly and adjust the vent, so there is minimal smoke and heat loss.

Depending on the cook time, you may need to add more coals and wood chips, to maintain heat. Try to do this at the same time as basting, to minimize interruption of the smoking process. I usually keep a small pile of hot coals burning and hot, ready for addition to the grill when needed.

When finished, the meat should be as well cooked as you would prepare it any other way. The color of the meat will take on a yellowish, then brownish tone. You may want to open the lid, and baste occasionally. Although basting is important to keep the meat juicy, don't lift the lid too often as this allows heat loss and you can add 15 min. cook time, each time the lid is raised.

Experiment. This can be done on any outdoor grill with a vented lid. The commercial smokers work well, but you can make your own for less than half the cost, to your own specs.

Baking in Mud and Grass

This technique is wonderful for the wilderness survival person, and is also an interesting and delicious way to prepare a meal on the trail. For the sake of discussion, I will use a chicken breast as the meat, with conventional produce.

We take some hardy individuals down the river on 'wilderness survival' trips, and they eat only what they catch. This is a preferred method for cooking and often produces meals like fresh walleye or catfish stuffed with fresh mushrooms and wild onions.

Prepare a small fire with a base of coals. Also prepare a mud mixture from any available dirt and water. Mud should be thick and firm.

Butterfly the chicken breast by making an incision with your knife as if you wanted to cut the chicken in half the thin way, like two pieces of bread. Just don't quite cut all the way through. Stuff the crevasse with suitable filling. Chopped onions, celery, mushrooms and peppers are all good this way. Apple slices are also a favorite ingredient. Spice to your taste.

Fold the chicken back together 'sandwiching' the stuffing. Wrap the meat carefully in fresh green grass and leaves. Use only grass and leaves that are familiar and are not poisonous. Wrap to a thickness of about 1 inch. Dip into the mud, and cover the grass in mud. Mud coating should be 1-2 inches thick, and completely enclose the grass and leaves.

Place directly on the coals of the fire and let cook for about an hour. You may turn the 'package' over after 30 minutes or so, but be careful so as not to break open the mud.

Remove from heat and carefully break open. Inspect for adequate doneness. If it is undercooked, you may wish to finish it off on the grill or on a hot rock.

This is a most wonderful way to cook as it seals in all the flavors and few if any of the leaves or grass really stick to the food.

Dehydrating Foods for the Trail

Some of the recipes to follow call for hamburger. You can bring it in cooled, as is routinely done, or dehydrate it prior to leaving. This process is most practical when away from refrigeration or proper cooling for extended periods, such as backpacking or rock climbing where weight is such a crucial issue.

The process is really no secret, is quite easy, and calls for no special tools, although a commercially sold dehydrator is nice.

Go pick up some flank steak or chuck roast, for leanness. Or get pre-ground burger, but pick extra lean. We are going for the lowest end fat content, because it's the fat that will go rancid and spoil the meat.

Pan fry the ground beef until cooked brown, and drain off as much grease as possible. Then, still in the colander, put it in the sink and run hot water over it. This will wash away the vast majority of the remaining grease. Be sure to let the hot water run for an extra minute to avoid drain clogs.

Spread the burger on a few layers of newspaper topped with a few paper towels. This should finish off the remainder of the grease. When cool and "dry" spread it onto baking pans. I lay mine out in 1/4 pound portions, to make camp recipes easier to figure.

Put the pans in your oven at 100-120°. This will probably be the lowest setting on your oven, or less. Test with a thermometer. After cooking for 6-8 hours, the meat should have darkened in color, finished drying out and be in hard little pieces resembling driveway gravel. Let 'meat gravel' cool, and seal in zip-lock bags. The individual portions can be tweaked to your specs. Go by this ... 1-cup burger gravel roughly equals 1 pound of original weight burger.

At camp, boil the gravel for 5-8 minutes, to re-hydrate, to original texture. This can be added to macaroni-n-cheese, burger helper, or any other camp recipe perfectly.

> "Food is our Common ground,
> a universal experience."
>
> ~ *James Beard* ~

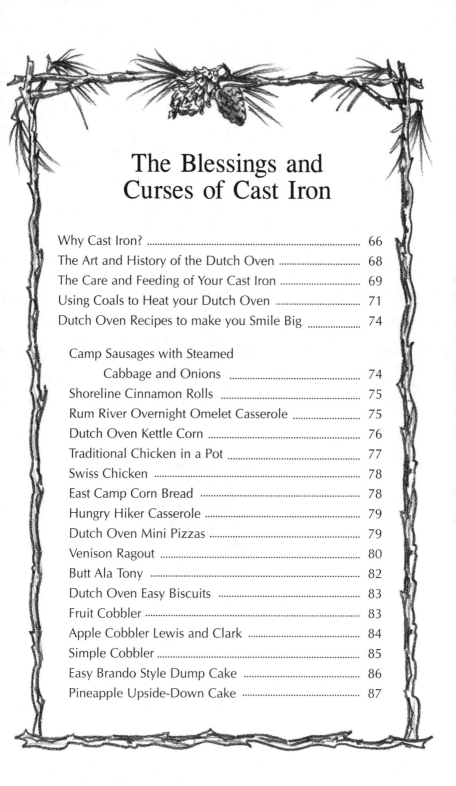

The Blessings and Curses of Cast Iron

Why Cast Iron? The Art and History of the Dutch Oven

First off, what is a Dutch Oven? A popular dictionary defines one as a heavy metal or enamelware pot with a high, arched lid.

Generally, I would describe a Dutch Oven as a cast iron or cast aluminum pot with a heavy lid, meant to be used either over an open fire, on a stovetop, or in an oven.

In fact, they really are more than an oven. They are a skillet, roaster, oven, soup kettle, and deep fryer, all in one.

When laid upside down on a bed of coals, a Dutch Oven lid becomes a nice wok-like frying pan, draining most of the grease away from the food, due to its' concave design.

When buried in a thick bed of coals, it becomes a great roaster for corn on the cob, and such. If hung over a nice hot fire, it becomes a great soup kettle!

If you lay it over a bed of hot coals, say 5-8 in number, and lay an additional 15-19 on the lid, it transforms itself into an oven worthy of any cornbread, cinnamon rolls, fruit cobbler, or sourdough!

For a nice frying surface, the oven can be laid upside down, with legs in the air (If it has legs). Lay coals on the bottom of the oven, then lay the upside down lid on the legs. There you have it! It's time for camp stir-fry, or grilled cheese, or you name it!

Furthermore, if you wanted to bake a pie, or cake, ready for after lunch, dig a shallow (2-3 inches deep) hole, the circumference of the oven. Lay down some foil, lining the hole, and place some good, hot coals on the foil, to cover it mostly. Either using a few small rocks, or a grate, create a surface on which to set the pie tin, or what have you, so that it will rest 3-4 inches above the coals.

Lay down the pie tin, or cake or bread or brownie pan. Cover the works with the inverted Dutch Oven. Proceed with your frying as mentioned above. Be sure to save room for dessert! (The dessert should take about as long as it would at home, in the kitchen.)

Ovens come in a variety of sizes: 3, 5, 8, 10, 12 and 14, up to 24-inch diameters. They run 4-10+ inches deep along the walls.

Dutch Ovens may also come with or without little attached legs, and with or without flat lids. This is what differentiates indoor ovens from outdoor ovens, although they can generally be inter-changeable.

The indoor types are legless and have rounded lids, without rims. The lack of legs makes it easy to use them stovetop. The out-door types have legs that make them easy to stack on each other, and to stand an inch or two high, just room enough for a layer of hot coals.

When several Dutch Ovens are used together, it is really effec-tive. The larger one goes on the bottom, with coals underneath the bottom and on top of the rimmed lid. The next is stacked on top, using the first ones lid coals as bottom coals, and so forth.

To see a master cook go to work with a full set of ovens is really impressive, and shows the simple marvel of the design of this oven. A pyramid shaped tower of ovens is quite a sight, and very heat effective.

Of course, safety dictates that caution should be used, *especially with young children around*, that the tower isn't knocked over.

They also are available in new-fangled cast-aluminum or tradi-tional cast iron. As far as I'm concerned, the cast-iron ones are the way to go. And having consulted with more than a few old-timers on the topic, they all seem to agree.

The cast iron versions have been tried, tested, proven, and tried again, some for well over a century. In the discussion of cast-iron cookery, it's not at all uncommon to hear of, or talk to, someone who still uses their great-great grandmother's old cast iron skillet or Dutch Oven! That's more than enough of a testimonial for me! The cast aluminum is likely to be less costly, but also is much more subject to warping in high heat, or rapid cooling. And when your investment will usually run $20-$35 for the good stuff, why not? If you are one who frequents auctions and such, they can sell for as low as $1!

A Bit of Dutch Oven History

Dutch Ovens are clearly not a new idea. They probably evolved from the huge cooking cauldrons used widely back as far as the 12th or 13th century. I suppose with the migratory habits of bands of people, they created smaller, more portable models. Certainly, in the relatively recent events such as the Westward Expansion of the U.S., they were carried in covered wagons, on pack mules, and aboard west-bound trains.

It's a fact that Meriwether Lewis and William Clark, on their journey across the young United States, listed their Dutch Ovens as being among their most prized equipment.

The history of the evolution of the Dutch Oven is rich to be sure; with stories of mining town celebrations, church socials, high-plains drifters, and cattle roundups, as well as countless others.

But for certain is the fact that from outdoorsmen to Boy Scouts, to gourmet cooks with a lunatic fringe, the Dutch Oven is still popular today.

These heavy iron utensils are still seen in camps everywhere that a little extra weight and bulk isn't a concern, and exceptional cooking is desired. They are still being used by those who can appreciate the versatility and dependability offered by these ovens.

Although (not surprisingly) not too popular with hikers due to their weight, they are perfect for camping, cabins, hunting camps, and backyard barbecues. Of course, the more uses you have for even a heavy, bulky item ... the more you can justify bringing it along!

They have even given us a new breed of ovens. There is an oven sold now that has a cone in the middle, similar to a bunt-cake pan.

The cone has slots in it, where heat from the coals can pass in and through, circulating hot air! It's like a little convection oven! There are also two levels of cook-space, as they provide two slotted shelves which slip down over the cone.

It works wonderfully! I have one and use it along with my other traditional ovens.

The Care and Feeding of Your Cast Iron

If you choose the cast iron Dutch Ovens you will need to season it before use, if you buy it new. Some of them are coated with a rust inhibitor, right at the factory. This waxy coating will need to be burned off. And it will smoke! Do not try to do this indoors. It should be laid atop a fire and left alone for 10 minutes or so to burn away the wax. Then wipe it out thoroughly and proceed to seasoning the pan as directed below.

The iron, in its' thickness, design, and very molecular makeup, is extremely efficient in distributing heat evenly, even on an imperfect campfire. They are also almost stick-proof. The trick here is to keep the pan well seasoned. This happens by applying oil to the surfaces of the oven when, or just prior to a time when, the oven will be exposed to heat.

I heard one time, that you could season a pan well by dropping it in a hot deep fryer and leaving it for a few minutes. This cooks the oil into the pores of the oven, not only helping to prevent stuck food, but also preventing rust.

But, since most of us don't always have access to a deep fryer, just heat the oven up, over coals or a stovetop. I add 2-3 inches of oil, and heat until the oil begins to splatter. Once the inside is done, I let the oil cool, pour from oven, and, using a paper towel, coat the outside with oil. Wipe off any oil that seems real excess, or that may be collecting in a puddle, and it's seasoned!

Don't try this indoors, as it will get quite smoky, and smelly. For indoors seasoning, I recommend a solid type shortening, such as Crisco. Once melted, rub on grease or oil with a soft cloth all over (the oven). (Although I've heard old timers say it will soften your skin.) Then put in a slow, low heat, 120 degrees or so, oven for an hour or so. I would certainly not recommend any type of animal grease for this. It will get rancid. (Come to think of it, a few of the old timers smelt a lot like rancid bacon grease.)

This should be done twice, to really accomplish good seasoning. The oven will develop a black patina when used for a while. The appearance has been compared to a black satin bowling ball.

If you use the oven to boil stew, or say, chili, it will need a booster seasoning. Water and any solution with high acidity (like tomatoes) will kind of 'suck' the oil from the iron. These 'boosters' will be needed occasionally, anyway.

Due to the very nature of the cast iron, only the most stubborn of burnt on foods will actually require scrubbing off. Especially if you just burn the scraps left behind longer. Just wipe with a wet cloth, and you're set. If there are real stubborn scraps left behind, like burnt-on pie filling, just scrape them off with a spoon or even a putty-knife. I carry a little grill brush that has a scraper on one side, works every time!

Now, the great debate:

To soap or not to soap? Since the pores full of oil are your seasoning, using soap to clean after each use would seem silly. The old timers say not to clean with soap, just a rag or wire brush, and lots of water. More modern convention would say to soap, and re-oil every time.

My opinion is – soap up once in a while, then re-oil. I have never had a health, or taste related problem due to not soaping.

Occasionally, (1-2 times per year) I will wash my ovens lightly with soap. More just to say that I do, than out of a health concern. I am careful to give the pan a good follow-up seasoning though.

You can make up your own mind about this debate.

However, regardless of how you wash, there is really only **one way to dry**.

Dump excess water out, and put the pot over a slow, steady heat. Let the heat *cook the moisture out* of the pores of the pan. When all visible moisture is gone, lightly but thoroughly swab the entire pot with a lightly oiled cloth.

Paper towels tend to 'shed', so I avoid them when possible. I keep an oiled cloth right in my pot when stored, to be used next time. You can get several uses out of a good rag.

We have a wood-burning stove in our living room as heat for the house. The hot top of the stove provides a great place to slow heat the Dutch Ovens. You could certainly use a low-fired conventional oven. Or setting it outside in the full sun on a hot day will open up the pores.

Necessary Equipment:

Using a Dutch Oven will require a few extra items, also. But luckily, most of these are either dirt cheap or easy to find around the house.

1. Heavy Leather Gloves. I have a nice, old pair of leather welding gloves that are my favorites.

2. Pliers. Come in handy for lifting, or turning a hot lid. You could also use a notched stick, or the claw of a hammer. You can also find 'lid lifters' for 3-5 dollars in stores that carry new Dutch Ovens.

3. A small whisk broom. This is real handy for sweeping off hot ashes, BEFORE removing the lid.

Using Coals to Cook with Dutch Ovens

How the oven is heated and for how long will (obviously) really affect its performance. Because of its design again, the oven will boil liquid from the bottom, yet bake from the top. Generally for baking the best rule of thumb as far as how many coals and where, is answered by a simple ratio.

Put about 18 large coals on the lid, and 6 or so under the oven. **This 3 to 1 ratio** is easy to remember, and pretty accurate. The **spacing of the coals** is the more important factor, due to the uneven heat derived from coals, or charcoal, although commercial charcoal is more predictable than wood coals. Just keep the coals spaced evenly, and you'll be fine.

Competitive Dutch Oven cookers stand over their ovens and occasionally rotate not only the lid a half turn, but also the bottom (in the opposite direction) for even heating and a perfect finish. Optimally, arrange the coals under the oven in a checkerboard pattern. When putting coals on top, arrange them in a circle around the outside rim, with one or two in the middle. The top ones in the circle will help to distribute heat evenly downward along the sides.

To re-distribute the heat, as a safeguard for some of the coals

fading away or heating up, just **give the lid a quarter, or half turn**, mid-way through. Generally, you'll be looking for an internal temperature of about 350°, if you follow these guidelines:
Here are a few basics to keep in mind:

I **RECOMMEND** laying your coals in a checkerboard type pattern on the bottom, and in a circle, with a few in the middle for on the lid.

BAKING: You'll need more heat from the top, than the bottom. Place charcoal under oven, and on the lid at a 1:3 ratio (the lid getting more). I recommend pre-heating not only the oven, but the lid, for best results.

ROASTING: Here, you'll heat the top and the bottom equally. Say, 12-14 on top, and the same, on the bottom.

FRYING AND BOILING: Here you'll provide heat from the bottom only. The heat will rise up the sides of the pan, so be sure to stir here. The lid all by itself can be used as a separate frying surface when placed directly on coals.

STEWING, SIMMERING: Ideally, almost all heat will come from the bottom. If the liquid is deep and cold, use the lid and add a few coals on top too.

I **ALSO RECOMMEND** using charcoal briquettes rather than wood-fire coals. They will last longer, and will be much more consistent in heat and duration. However, some prefer wood. Hardwoods will provide the best wood coals possible.

Another hint: *Don't ever add cold water to a hot oven.* This may seem elementary, but I've heard stories. Needless to say, this may very well crack your oven.
Yet another hint: each coal the size of a charcoal briquette, of equal doneness, will add about 10-20 degrees.
The coal or charcoal briquette, to be at optimum effectiveness for cooking should glow from within a light coat of gray ash that has been described as looking like a light coat of gray flannel.
It is certainly not wise to add extra coals to speed up the cooking time, you'll just end up increasing the chance of burnt food.

Still another hint: If you are going to place another dish, or pan inside the Dutch oven, I recommend allowing a bit of air space between the two surfaces, top and bottom.

A great way to do this is to ball up 5 medium pieces of tin foil. Place four of them in the center of the oven, in a circle the size of the pan used. Put the last one in the center of the others, and lay pan on top. You may want to apply a bit of weight to the pan at this time, to flatten the balls slightly. These are re-useable and give you about an inch of great air circulation under the interior pan.

A good option to foil balls is to use canning jar rings. Even small rocks would work – you get the idea.

The toughest part for me is to avoid the temptation of peeking at the food while it cooks. Yes, there are many valid excuses to justify this, but accept the fact that if you lift the lid during cooking, the hot air or steam that your oven is working so hard to retain, will be lost. The cook-time, and possibly the appearance (esp. if baking) of the food will be vulnerable to change.

Either follow a recipe, or put your faith in your instincts … but don't peek! Really, for best results, use an oven thermometer ahead of time and experiment to see how your particular oven heats.

When baking in your Dutch oven, you may opt to pour the batter directly into the hot oven, or use another pan that will fit inside. Just make sure to use a pan small enough that it isn't tight or you may not get it out.

In Summary

Cooking with a Dutch Oven is a wonderful skill, and a lot of fun to practice. Start out with something fairly basic, and get to know your oven. It won't be long, before you are amazing friends and family alike with this unique, awesome tool.

Let's start out the section with one of the most simple, easy-to-make recipes, for Dutch Oven cooking.

This is not only the most elementary of recipes, but also one of the quickest, cheapest, and certainly a time proven favorite. My brother, even having had many a camp meal that was far more 'gourmet', sang its praises on a recent camping trip in the mountains.

Dutch Oven Recipes to Make You Smile Big

CAMP SAUSAGE AND STEAMED CABBAGE WITH ONIONS

1	medium/large yellow onion, peeled, and sliced
1	head fresh cabbage, washed, and chopped lg.
1	ring sausage, or Kielbasa, 'ready to eat'-type
11/2-2	cups water

This recipe could also easily be made in a large cast iron skillet, with either a safe lid, or some tin foil, tightly wrapped.

Begin by placing the sliced onion in the pan, to cover the bottom. Next, add a layer of chopped cabbage, about 2-3 inches deep over the onion. Place the sausage or Kielbasa in the center of the pan or oven, on the cabbage. Add another layer of cabbage, to cover the sausage. Pour in the water, and add spices, as you desire. A bit of salt and pepper, with a dash of garlic powder is great.

Now, either put on the lid (for Dutch Ovens), or wrap the pan in several layers of tin foil. Just be sure that the seal is relatively tight. Place on a grill, or large rocks, to the side of the fire, and begin warming over medium heat. After 15 or so minutes, pull a few more coals under the pot, and cook for another 20 minutes, to a half-hour. The heat here should be medium, to medium high. At least 15 minutes prior to eating, you should be able to hear the water simmering inside, then followed by steam escaping the pan, if you are using foil.

Remove from heat, lift away lid, and serve. This recipe could easily be doubled or tripled, if you have a pot to accommodate. Just layer the ingredients, their flavors really cook together well. Don't try to save time by pre-cutting sausage. This just releases all their juices, and dries them out.

Due to boiling water, there should be little involved in cleanup here. But, your Cast Iron will need a booster seasoning after a meal like this.

RUM RIVER OVERNIGHT OMELET CASSEROLE

6-8   fresh eggs, beaten with a splash of water
      Sausage or bacon of choice
6-8   slices bread, cubed (the size of acorns)
  1   can mushroom or celery soup
2/3   cup milk or water
  1   cup shredded cheese of choice
      Spices to taste

In a casserole, pie pan, loaf pan, or foil lined Dutch Oven, brown the meat until done and separate from grease. Return meat to pan, chopping it with a spoon or spatula if necessary. Add bread cubes and spread evenly across the meat crumbles. Add egg mixture, pouring evenly over the top. Mix soup and 2/3 cup milk or water, then add to mix. Let this sit covered and refrigerated overnight preferably, or for 1 hour at least. Uncover when ready to cook. Sprinkle cheese evenly over the mixture. Bake at medium heat (about 325°) for about one hour, or until cooked through. Cooking time will vary with the depth of mixture – the deeper, the longer it will take.

This is an awesome camp breakfast that can be mostly assembled the night before, easing the cooking duties in the morning.

SHORELINE CINNAMON ROLLS

These are awesome and easy in the morning! Please refer to the breakfast section of the book for cooking instructions.

DUTCH OVEN KETTLE CORN

1 **large Dutch Oven**
1 **cup water**
8 **ears fresh sweet corn**
   Salt, butter, pepper, and other spices
   (to taste)

Remove the husks and silk from corn, separating the husks as you go. Trim away any scrubby ends or rotten parts.

You should have a fire going, with a nice bed of coals, 4 or so inches thick.

Using the husks, completely, and generously line the bottom and insides of oven. Break corn ears in half, and pile them in the central area of the oven. Making sure the bottom, and sides have husks about 1 1/2 inches thick, cover the top of the corn with remainder of husks. Add water to the oven and put lid on tightly.

The weight of the lid itself should be heavy enough to keep steam in.

Slide your oven onto the coals, so there is a border of coals around pot. Take either loose coals or a burning log from fire and lay on top of oven.

Timing is the key to this easy recipe, and there is NO foolproof method. The corn should take about 15-20 minutes to cook completely. This will vary with density of the corn and husks, as well as with the heat of the fire, and size of the oven.

Remove from fire, and carefully (so as to avoid steam burns) remove the lid of the oven. Take out the corn, eat and enjoy.

This is definitely the consummate method of corn preparation! For an even greater flavor, try this. Before " lidding" the oven add, ABOVE the husks, a scrap piece of corn.

This bit will char slightly and lend a wonderful, smoky essence! This is eatin'!

TRADITIONAL CHICKEN IN A POT

1   whole fryer, dressed, washed, patted dry
3   red potatoes, washed, and quartered
3   carrots, washed and peeled
1   Tbs. fresh chopped basil
    Salt and pepper
1   Tbs. 'poultry magic', 'Lawrys' or other similar
    seasoning

Sprinkle cavity (the chickens) with salt and pepper, lightly. Lay vegetables in cavity. Place chicken in oven. Sprinkle with seasoning, and basil. Cover and bake for 2-3 hours, using heat guide for Dutch Ovens, given at the start of this chapter.

Chicken is done, when juices run clear, not cloudy, and meat is white, not pink, ALL THE WAY TO THE BONE. Test cut into the deepest meat, to the bone. (Thigh, or breast.) The internal temperature of the meat, next to the bone should be 375°.

You could certainly add a touch of water, and add more vegetables around the chicken. A simple, delicious feast for 3-4 adults!

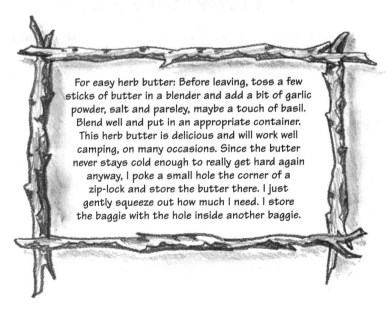

For easy herb butter: Before leaving, toss a few sticks of butter in a blender and add a bit of garlic powder, salt and parsley, maybe a touch of basil. Blend well and put in an appropriate container. This herb butter is delicious and will work well camping, on many occasions. Since the butter never stays cold enough to really get hard again anyway, I poke a small hole the corner of a zip-lock and store the butter there. I just gently squeeze out how much I need. I store the baggie with the hole inside another baggie.

SWISS CHICKEN

This is a very simple, very delicious recipe.

    6 **oz. chicken breasts or thigh cutlets**
        (boneless skinless)
        Several slices Swiss cheese
    1 **can cream of chicken soup**
  1/3 **cup water**

Lay chicken breasts out flat in a shallow pan. Season to taste with a bit of salt, pepper, garlic.

Mix soup and water together, and pour over chicken.

Lay out cheese slices over the chicken.

Cover, and bake at 350° for 30-45 minutes.

The cheese will be bubbly, melted and delicious over the top of these juicy pieces of chicken. Easy, easy, easy, and good, good, good!

EAST CAMP CORNBREAD

Mix all ingredients well. Pour into Dutch Oven, or pan in Dutch

    1 **can kernel corn**
    1 **can creamed corn**
    6 **oz. sour cream**
    1 **stick butter, or margarine**
    1 **egg**
    1 **package Jiffy cornbread muffin mix**

Oven, and bake for 35-40 minutes, with 6 or 7 coals on the bottom, and on top. Mmmmmmm!

HUNGRY HIKER CASSEROLE

This is one of my dear mother's most requested dishes. She always prepared it for me on special occasions. It is also great over a fire, and quite simple to prepare.

1/4 cup chopped onion
1 Tbs. oil
1 lb. lean ground beef
2 lb. cans pork-n-beans
1/4 cup catsup
1/4 cup water
1/2 tsp. garlic salt
1/4 cup brown sugar
optional, 1 can biscuits, pop-open-type

Sauté onion in oil, add ground beef, and cook until browned, drain. Pour beans into a medium Dutch Oven, or pot. Add ground beef and onions. Stir in catsup, water, and garlic salt. Sprinkle with brown sugar. Lid, and bake for 15-20 minutes, at about 375°.

Top with biscuits, and increase heat to about 475° (add coals to top). Bake ten more minutes lidded, until biscuits are golden. Top with shredded cheese.

DUTCH OVEN MINI PIZZAS

2 English muffins, sliced open
1 cup tomato or pizza sauce
1 cup shredded cheese, cheddar

Simply spread a thick layer of tomato, or pizza sauce on each half muffin, and top with cheese, portioning it out equally. You can jazz this up, obviously, with chopped black olives, mushrooms, sausage bits, or other favorite pizza toppings, under cheese.

Place on a plate, or tin, in Dutch Oven, cover, and bake for 10-12 minutes, 5-8 coals under, and 15 or so on top. Gooey, and good. Also another favorite for the kids, big and small.

AN OLD WORLD DUTCH OVEN RECIPE
VENISON RAGOUT

It's easy to sense the history in this variation of a classic recipe that has been around for perhaps hundreds of years. Many versions of the Old World recipes for this dish were prepared with deer blood in the sauce as a thickening agent. This is a reflection of the peasants use of every part of an animal, and I'm sure would lend certain richness to the sauce.

But, since deer blood doesn't retain its freshness well, and I'm not sure what kind of response it would get, we'll just go with this more contemporary version, still every bit a timeless classic.

And it's truly a dish that cries out to be prepared in a Dutch Oven. Modified, yes it may be made with beef, inside, on the stove, with delicious results.

Every fall, I start to crave this dish. It always brings to mind cool autumn weekends, leaves of all kinds exploding with color, friends in warm flannel shirts around an open fire, sharing a bottle or two of a warming red wine.

3	lbs. venison, of any cut, in 1-inch pieces
3	Tbs. cream butter
3/4	lb. fresh button mushrooms, halved
10	small white onions, peeled and medium diced
3/4	cup beef or venison stock
5-6	Tbs. tomato paste
2 1/2	cups burgundy table wine
1/4	cup dry sherry
4	Tbs. white flour
1	tsp. granulated garlic
1/2	tsp. ground black pepper
2-3	bay leaves

Place, or hang over medium hot coals, your Dutch Oven, or use stockpot over medium heat. Melt butter, and add venison pieces. Brown these lightly. Remove venison from pan and add onions and mushrooms, cooking briefly until tender, and the onions are transparent. Remove these from pot.

Stir in beef stock and tomato paste. In a separate bowl, combine wine, sherry, and flour, and stir rapidly, to a light pasty liquid. Add this mixture to the pot and heat. Once mixture is very hot, add other ingredients, cover tightly and cook over medium heat for 1 1/2 hours. At end of time, remove lid and taste for tenderness of venison. It should be deliciously tender, and full of flavor. This dish makes its own gravy, and would traditionally be served over spatzle, but I actually prefer a light bed of mashed potatoes, with homemade bread as an accompaniment. You could certainly substitute most any short, soft pasta, or thick cubes of homemade bread, for the spatzle (a dumpling-like noodle.)

BUTT ALA TONY

Perfect for the autumn yard party! This is a time-tested favorite, that I'm positive will earn you much praise.

```
  5  lb. pork butt
  2  sweet potatoes, firm but ripe
  2  red apples, cored, and sliced thick
3/4  cup flour
1/2  cup brown sugar
  1   Tbs. ground cinnamon
1/4  cup bacon drippings
3/4  cup Bourbon (1/4 cup of which is on ice with a splash
     of water, for the cook)
     Spices, to taste
```

Heat up drippings, in a large Dutch Oven over a medium heat.

Roll the pork in flour, and season appropriately. Lay the meat in hot grease, and roll it around, searing all sides. The meat could be scored prior to searing – for flavor. ('Scoring' is different now than it was in high school. It is to make long, shallow cuts in the meat, usually prior to cooking, seasoning or marinade. Cuts may be in a criss-cross manner, or how you wish, around the entirety of meat.)

When browned, move oven to a spot emitting medium-low heat.

Add other ingredients, except flour and the cooks ration of bourbon. Place lid on tightly, and cook about 1 1/2 hours.

Test center of meat for doneness before serving. Some ingredients will have stuck to the pan, so remove to serving dish, place empty Dutch Oven over high heat, and de-glaze with wine, stock, or other liquid for gravy. (If unfamiliar with de-glazing ... that is the method in which burnt, or stuck food is loosened by adding cool liquid, and stirred over high heat. A thickener may be added, if desired.)

DUTCH OVEN BISCUITS

Using commercially pre-mixed dough or your own recipe, proceed as follows.

Oil the oven, both the bottom and the sides. Coat the oiled surface with a light dusting of flour. Assemble the mix (1/4 cup water, per cup mix).

Lightly coating your hands in flour will help prevent dough sticking to them. Roll the dough into little 'cookies' 2-3 inches wide, and 1 deep. Set these into pan, spacing them evenly.

Cover the oven, and cook over hot coals, rotating occasionally, to prevent hot spots. Cook 7-10 minutes.

FRUIT COBBLER

This was a standard fare during my young days as a Boy Scout. It would seem that no summer camp evening was complete without cobbler before bed. This recipe is using canned cherry pie filling, but you could certainly use other flavors, and varieties, of fruit.

- 2 **cups of biscuit mix**
- 2 **cups white sugar**
- 2 **cups milk, room temp.**
- 1 **cup shortening**
- 1 **pint of cherry pie filling**

Mix all ingredients; pour into a well-greased pan, or directly into Dutch Oven. Cover with lid, and bake 45 minutes to an hour, using above ratio for coals. Serve, perhaps, with ice cream.

This is only one version of cobbler, and one approach to its construction. Most recipes will say to put filling on the bottom of pan, and cover with some type of crust. The following recipe uses just this technique, with a twist: its apple crisp, not cobbler.

APPLE COBBLER LEWIS AND CLARK

2	cans apple pie filling
1/2	half cup chopped nuts

Topping:

1 1/2	cup white flour
1/2	cup rolled oats, instant oatmeal
1/4	tsp. salt
1/2	cup brown sugar
1/2	cup white sugar
10	Tbs. butter (soft)

Pour filling into a well seasoned Dutch oven (12"). In a bowl, mix flour, oats, salt, and sugars together, then stir in butter. Dump on filling, cover, and bake for 1 hour. You may want to check it once or twice for burning, and rotate to prevent any hot spots. Serve it up, and kick your feet back, loosen the belt a notch, and enjoy.

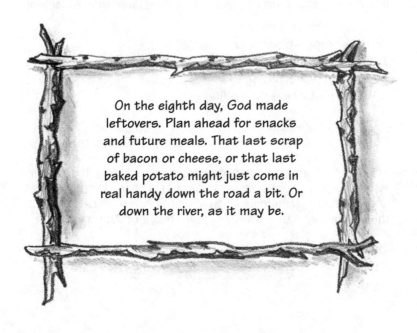

On the eighth day, God made leftovers. Plan ahead for snacks and future meals. That last scrap of bacon or cheese, or that last baked potato might just come in real handy down the road a bit. Or down the river, as it may be.

SIMPLE COBBLER

As its name implies, this one is almost too easy. This is an old scouting recipe that has been the pride of many new campers to show their parents on Lodge Night.

Its ease and interest to kids is comparable to the Notso Hotdog recipe that follows later.

1   **12 ounce can fruit pie filling, your favorite (cherry or blueberry are great)**
1   **box white or yellow cake mix; plain, no pudding, etc. White is best.**
1   **12 oz. can lemon lime soda**

Pour filling in the bottom of Dutch Oven (you may wish to foil line this one.) Spread out evenly with spoon or spatula. Sprinkle cake mix evenly over the top. Pour most of the can of soda over the top. DO NOT MIX OR STIR.

Bake over medium heat for 45-60 minutes.

This is a lemony treat that will be crunchy around the edges, and chewy in the middle.

"When I let go of what I am,
I become what I might be."

~ *Lao Tzu* ~

ANOTHER EASY CAMP COBBLER – BRANDY'S DUMP CAKE

25-30	ounces sliced, canned peaches, in syrup
1	small can crushed pineapple
6 to a dozen	Maraschino cherries (optional)
1	box yellow, or white cake mix
2-3	Tbs. butter, or margarine
	A cold slab of good vanilla ice cream

Easy, easy, easy! Dump in the fruits. Dump in the cake mix. Spread evenly across fruit. Dump in little blobs of butter, spaced evenly, across mix.

Put the lid on the Dutch Oven and begin to cook with a dozen or so coals underneath and as many, or a few more on top, say 16 or so.

Try to keep the kids occupied for 40-45 minutes, until the cake is browned. You may wish to rotate the oven occasionally to prevent hot spots. Serve with a big hunk of vanilla ice cream, and enjoy!

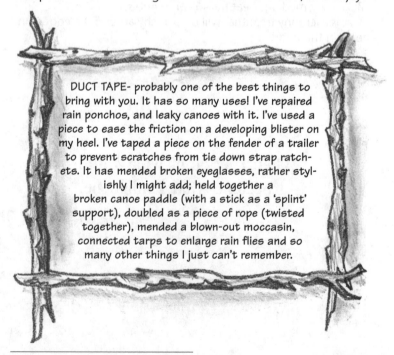

DUCT TAPE- probably one of the best things to bring with you. It has so many uses! I've repaired rain ponchos, and leaky canoes with it. I've used a piece to ease the friction on a developing blister on my heel. I've taped a piece on the fender of a trailer to prevent scratches from tie down strap ratchets. It has mended broken eyeglasses, rather stylishly I might add; held together a broken canoe paddle (with a stick as a 'splint' support), doubled as a piece of rope (twisted together), mended a blown-out moccasin, connected tarps to enlarge rain flies and so many other things I just can't remember.

PINEAPPLE UPSIDE-DOWN CAKE – DUTCH OVEN STYLE

This recipe comes from my brother. He made it riverside on the Niobrara River during a memorable canoe trip. It's super easy, but is a great dessert at camp, especially for a birthday or other special occasion.

  1 **box yellow cake mix**
 10 **Maraschino cherries**
  1 **can sliced pineapple rings (10 slices and juice)**
1/4 **cup butter**
  3 **eggs**
1/3 **cup vegetable oil**
1/2 **cup brown sugar**

Preheat a 12-inch Dutch Oven with about 8 coals underneath, and about 18 on top.

In a mixing bowl or large baggie combine cake mix, eggs, oil, and pineapple juice. Stir just until lumps are gone. If more liquid is needed, use a bit of the cherry juice. Set mix aside.

Melt butter and brown sugar in Dutch Oven, stirring until dissolved consistently. Place pineapple rings evenly in the bottom of oven. Place a cherry inside each ring.

Pour cake batter evenly over the rings.

Return heated lid to oven and bake approximately 35 minutes or until a toothpick inserted into middle of cake comes out clean. Be sure to rotate lid and bottom occasionally to prevent hot spots.

When the cake is done, remove the lid and immediately invert the cake onto a serving platter or foil. Be sure to watch the bail handle on the oven to avoid damaging the cake in the process.

This is great served with ice cream! (Recipe for this in dessert section of book.)

Be a good example. Practice what you preach, and preach what you practice. Teach others who don't know the right way. Ignorance is catchy - the right way takes effort.

~ *Anonymous* ~

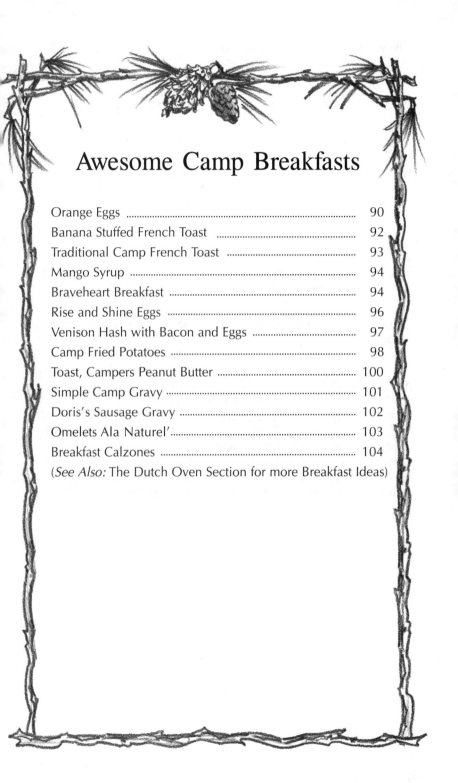

Awesome Camp Breakfasts

(*See Also:* The Dutch Oven Section for more Breakfast Ideas)

GREAT ORANGE PEEL EGGS

This easy breakfast has been a favorite amongst my friends and family for years! The delicate essence of the orange is poached into the egg. Not enough to flavor, mind you- just an essence.

It also requires no plate or bowl, which can be a plus in the morning. This recipe is a must for you to try.

Per Person:

1 **large navel orange (thick skinned)**
2 **fresh eggs**
  One 4x4 piece of foil

Cut orange in symmetrical halves, and have the appetizer by scooping out the juicy fruit, and eating it with a spoon (grapefruit style) without disturbing the little stem-nipple thing in the middle.

Crack the eggs into the empty orange half. Carefully cover the open end with the foil. Place the orange (foil up!) on the edge of the fire, on top of some gently hot coals. You may wish to pick up a small (cherry-sized) coal and lay it atop the foil for a minute or two. Leave for 10-12 minutes, and remove. Take off the foil, and ... Presto! Great, easy eggs, ala orange!

You can use the other half-orange peeling to act as a sleeve, with which to hold the hot half. This, along with a little fried bacon and a cup of hot coffee or cocoa, is the perfect way to start your day!

Thicker skinned oranges work for this far superior to the thin ones. The same technique works excellent for baking gingerbread or cookie dough in the fire. (Just sub cookie dough or gingerbread for the eggs!)

Or, for a different approach to the egg idea, you could substitute one hollowed half red onion, for the orange. And the top half would make a great top while cooking. Put hamburger in the 1/2 onion for dinner.

Yet another variation is to place a piece of ham betwixt the foil and the eggs. The little coal on top works good here.

- Ramen types of dishes are quick, easy, and leave little or no cleanup. They are even better if you add chopped scallions, peppers, canned de-boned chicken, etc. Just decrease the water called for in the instructions, if you want more of pasta, than soup.

- For hassle free bacon- drape it over a piece of wire or a Dutch oven handle-and slow cook over the fire. The grease will run off, the bacon shrivels less, and there's no mess. Cook slowly and watch for flare-ups from the grease.

BANANA STUFFED FRENCH TOAST

This is a great recipe for home or at camp! It's pretty simple, and the results are great! It has become a favorite at camp, with the adults and kids alike.

1	loaf bread, *un-sliced*
2	bananas, peeled and sliced (the long way works best, I think)
3	cup soft butter
3/4	large eggs, whipped with the following ingredients:
1/2	cup milk
1	tsp. vanilla extract
	pinch each of cinnamon, and nutmeg

Slice the bread, discarding the end pieces, as follows. Cut all the way through the first time, and only 3/4-way through the next. All the way through the third, and so on. Each slice should be a total of about 3/4-inch thick.

Stuff the crevice in each piece with a few of the banana slices.
Carefully dip this into the egg wash mixture.

Lay in a buttered, hot pan. Leave for 2 min, or until one side is browned to your taste, then flip over, and repeat.

Serve with your favorite topping, syrup, powdered sugar, honey, or whatever.

FRENCH TOAST ON THE GRILL, WITH MANGO SYRUP

Serves Four

8	thick slices bread, country-style
6	large fresh eggs
1/2	tsp. cinnamon
	Dash nutmeg
1/2	tsp. sugar
1/2	tsp. vanilla extract
1/4	cup milk
4	Tbs. butter
	(may sub. bacon drippings)

Over a bed of hot coals, lay a skillet to pre-heat.

Combine eggs, spices, sugar, vanilla extract, and milk. Beat these together, using a whisk, or two forks. (Press the handles together, as in a drawer, more beat for the buck.)

Once beaten well, begin dunking the bread in mixture. Allow to sit for a moment to somewhat soak a little.

Place pieces on the hot, buttered pan and let each side brown.

Texture should be firm, but springy when done. Served with Mango Syrup, they're unbeatable!

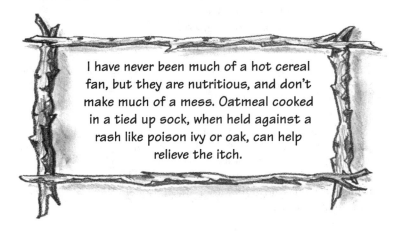

I have never been much of a hot cereal fan, but they are nutritious, and don't make much of a mess. Oatmeal cooked in a tied up sock, when held against a rash like poison ivy or oak, can help relieve the itch.

MANGO SYRUP

Serves Four

2   **ripe mangoes. Ripe when slightly red/orange in color, and a bit soft.**
1/4   **cup honey, warm**
    Dash cinnamon

Peel the mangoes, and discard peeling. Chop the fruit as fine as possible, then stir vigorously, perhaps mashing with a fork. (If at home, puree in food processor.)

When they are as near smooth as possible, add remainder of ingredients, and stir some more. Warm slightly, as breakfast is prepared. Pour over French toast, or pancakes, or any pastry.

I guarantee your guests will clean up any excess! Also makes an awesome sauce to rub over cooked pork or chicken.

BRAVEHEART BREAKFAST

Per Person:

2   **fresh eggs**
4   **slices bacon**
1   **med. paper sack**
    Lots of patience, and
    Huge sense of humor

My mother taught us this one on a camping trip when I was very young. It certainly sounds like a crazy thing to attempt. The family dog was very well-fed that morning, by our failed attempts to learn this one.

I don't recommend experimenting with this one, if you can't afford to lose a few portions. But, if you approach it with a sense of humor, it's a fun test of luck, patience and skill.

The general idea is to open the sack, and lay out bacon flat on the bottom of it. Close bag, by folding it neatly at the top, in several one-inch folds.

Poke a sharp hot-dog stick through the sack just below the seam. Hold sack, with stick, carefully over coals. I would recommend starting high, and coming down as you go.

After the bacon has started cooking, it will begin to grease the bottom of the sack.

At this point, set the bag on the ground, open it and crack in the eggs on top of the bacon. Refold bag, re-insert stick and commence cooking.

You will have to be very patient, and slow cook the eggs, but I HAVE SEEN this done successfully! Of course I have also seen many, many flaming bags hit the ground!

This is a fun one for scout troops, and groups of kids in general. Just have a backup plan for the majority, who, if not very careful, will lose out. A hungry dog for cleanup doesn't hurt either!

For the skilled hotshot in the group, bonus points for impaling a piece of bread on the end of stick, and making toast out of it, while cooking eggs!

Have fun!

Also, this method can work for cooking other foods. The bacon on the bottom is the secret. Try freshly caught fish this way, it's awesome. (Once you've mastered the technique, of course.)

RISE AND SHINE EGGS

This wonderful breakfast meal or variations of it, are often served at brunch. It is quite easy to prepare and is just as delicious as it looks!

I served this to a group of corporate businessmen while on a trip along the Niobrara River in northern Nebraska and they absolutely marveled at the way the flavors meld together. They requested that on future trips, this breakfast be included in the menu at least one time. This one's for you guys!

Commercially prepared egg mix works great for this meal and eliminates the chance of broken eggshells.

1	**dozen eggs**
1	**pound chopped ham**
1	**bunch fresh asparagus spears, trimmed and chopped**
1/4	**cup minced shallots**
	Spices to taste
	Grated cheese to garnish, if desired

I like to prepare this dish in a non-stick casserole dish, but you could also cook it right in a Dutch Oven and it will turn out wonderfully.

Simply mix all ingredients and add to Dutch Oven that has been sprayed with vegetable oil spray. Put lid on Dutch Oven. Set oven on top of a few (3-5) coals, and put 8-10 coals on lid. Cook for 15-25 minutes. Every 3-5 minutes, rotate the bottom part as well as the lid, to prevent any hot spots.

Another way to cook is to use the 'dangle' method I speak of in the 'alternative cooking methods' section. Simply hang oven from a rope or chain over the coals. Add coals to lid as directed above, then swing the oven back and forth (gently over the fire).

VENISON HASH WITH BACON AND EGGS

There's just nothing like a bit of hash, to start the day off right!

Serves Six

3	Tbs. butter
1	lg. onion, finely diced
2	stalks celery
1	clove garlic, minced
1/2	green pepper, diced
3	large potatoes, boiled, and diced
1	Tbs. salt
1	Tbs. black pepper
1/3	cup heavy whipping cream
1 1/2	Tbs. Worcestershire sauce
1 1/2	pounds cold venison roast, diced

Melt butter in a deep cast iron skillet over hot coals or med. high heat and lightly brown the onions, green pepper, and celery.

Add the potatoes and stir frequently for 2-3 minutes more.

Add the venison and garlic, and continue for an additional 2-3 minutes.

Add salt and pepper, heavy cream, and Worcestershire sauce. Reduce the heat, and simmer covered, until some of the liquid has cooked away and hash is thicker.

On the grill or a separate pan, fry up the bacon the way you like it, and set aside to drain excess grease. Keeping about 4 Tbs. of grease in hot pan, carefully crack in 6 eggs, add 2 Tbs. water, and cover. Cook eggs to desired doneness, carefully remove, and lay over the hash mixture.

Lay bacon pieces around inside circumference of pan, and serve.

SHORELINE CINNAMON ROLLS

This isn't a scratch recipe, but you can make the rolls from scratch if you desire. For ease and those who are less experienced at baking, I include this idea as is, just because warm, fresh cinnamon rolls are awesome in the morning.

Buy a pop-open-type tube of cinnamon rolls. Follow the instructions on the tube, and place in a Dutch Oven.

If desired, use a greased round tin or pie plate, and follow the baking instructions listed in the Dutch Oven Section. Be careful not to use too much heat from the bottom, only 3-5 coals underneath needed and 8-10 on top.

They will only take about 20 minutes to cook, and if you have more than one Dutch Oven, you can stagger the start times for additional batches. I personally recommend slightly undercooking the rolls. These are sublimely easy and it seems that I can never make enough. They cook to steamy hot perfection over the coals, and everyone is always willing to have 'just one more'.

CAMP FRIED POTATOES

These babies are an essential component to every camp, be it a hunting shack, a summer canoe camp, or a lazy-weekend stay outdoors during a beautiful Indian Summer. And they're not half bad, prepared in your kitchen at home.

Breakfast anywhere is a hard thing to beat, I think. The sun rising, dew on the grass, a fresh pot of hot, strong coffee ... is the start of a great day right there. Let me get sidetracked for a moment (I think it's too late anyway).

The late great **Louis Lamour** wrote some great fodder for camp reading. One of the many classic phrases he used in one of his books described a character's coffee tastes.

The man liked his camp coffee "as black and hot as the hinges of Hell." I always thought that was a good description.

Anyway, back to Camp Fried Potatoes:

Here's the original backwoods recipe. Let me tell you, this is the real thing. You can vary yours as you please.

Halve, then slice one large potato per person served. Add two more for the dogs. This is also the best way to use up any leftover baked potatoes. Actually, I prefer to go this route, as it takes less time to cook, and they tend to crumble apart nicely.

Slice 1/4 medium yellow onion per person served.

Lay out 1/2 to 3/4 pound bacon slices in a medium-hot cast iron skillet. No need to peel them all apart, just put some fire to them.

Grab a mug of coffee and go outside. Find a slightly crooked stick about 8 inches long. (Bark is optional.) Have a few pulls of coffee, while enjoying the morning air; perhaps stretch a bit.

Go back in and using the cleanest end of the stick, give the bacon a stir.

Note that some folks prefer to save and reuse their bacon sticks if they find a real dandy.

When the bacon is done, remove from heat, and pour the grease over the dog food dish, reserving a few tablespoons in the pan. Set the bacon on a towel to drain.

Add the sliced potatoes and onions to the pan and cook till they're browned. If you wish, you can use your bacon stick to stir them, or find a different one. They'll start to soften and crumble slightly as they get cooked. Once browned on both sides thoroughly, remove from heat.

Crumble or break up the bacon that you haven't eaten while cooking. Stir this into the mix. If desired, you could add some grated cheese on top.

If you find yourself without a proper cheese grater, you could do as some of the mountain folk still do, and just poke nail-holes in a strong piece of tin. Use the rough side to grate the cheese.

Come to think of it, if you have to be told which side of the tin to shred with … stick to cereal and milk.

TOAST

This is, for my family, a staple at breakfast. There are all sorts of fancy ideas, and neat contraptions to do this, but come on, it's toast!

To tell the truth, most of my family loves toast with peanut butter so much that the quality of the toast has often been overlooked, as it is just a delivery vehicle for the peanut butter!

I just take a few pieces of bread, and lay them either on the coals directly, or sometimes prop them up on a rock, facing the heat. Wait a minute or so, remove from heat, blow off any ash, and chow down, or apply liberal amounts of peanut butter.

If a grill has already been set up for use for breakfast, I may opt to lay the bread on the grill for a minute or two. One can also use a stick to roast the toast over a fire until browned.

Additionally, by buttering the bread and laying it on a hot skillet, it will brown.

SPEAKING OF PEANUT BUTTER

If you are camping, or doing other vigorous activity, it's my opinion that you may want to increase your caloric intake, as well as complex carbohydrates, to compensate for extra energy spent. This becomes rule if winter camping, where your body will constantly burn much more fuel, just to keep warm.

Aside from all the good excuses that I may have, this just tastes great, and saves a step in the morning.

Before leaving, I have a special peanut butter that I mix for camping. It's simply commercial P.B., mixed with softened butter. I whip this all together, and the P.B. is deliciously smooth, and creamy. It is also extra rich. Not necessarily any more healthy, but I work a lot harder camping and the extra calories don't bother me.

OTHER SPREADABLES

We always pack in some other spreadable goodies, for variety. Jam or honey makes a great quick snack, with some bread. It will also come in real handy, when you want to give some back-country B.B.Q. ribs extra flair (used as a glaze), or meet a fellow camper, and over the course of sharing some morning coffee, find that even though you don't care for sweetener, they do. It's great to be able to offer some honey.

And if you are winter camping, or want some extra calories (it does happen from time to time) some honey, or maple syrup, or even jelly mixed with water, will make a sweet drink that will pep you up.

CAMP GRAVY

The easiest way is this. Using a fork, stir a bit of flour into some cold water, making a thin, runny paste. Heat up pan drippings, left from cooking meat, and stir the paste into the boiling drippings.

Stir rapidly, and let the gravy thicken. If it doesn't, add more paste.

If you de-glaze the pan first, with a splash of wine, juice, beer, or whatever, it will give you the essence of any bits of meat that may have stuck to the pan, thus making a better gravy, and an easier pan to clean

Any alcohol in the liquid will cook away in just a minute or two of simmering.

DORIS'S SAUSAGE GRAVY

My Grandma Doris is remembered for many things. Aside from being an awesome Grandma, she made the worlds greatest caramel rolls, pecan pie, and potato salad, to name a few things.

One favorite that was the eye opener many mornings was her biscuits and sausage gravy. She was a Southern Gal you see, being raised up in Oklahoma and Texas. Those people just plain know how to cook! And there was nothing plain about her cooking.

Here's the best adaptation of her sausage gravy that I could muster. It's not right on as she made it, but it's close enough.

3/4	lb. bulk ground sausage, or patties
1/4	cup flour (all purpose)
2	cups milk, or half 'n half
1/4	Tbs. ground black pepper
	Extra salt, or butter if you like; try it as is first.

In a cast iron skillet, thoroughly brown the sausage over medium heat. Of course, you could use a Dutch Oven, or adapt to what you have handy.

When cooked, drain off all but 1/2 cup sausage drippings. Save this in the skillet. Place skillet back on heat, and set aside the sausage to cool.

When drippings are bubbling, stir in the flour with a fork. It is okay to use your bacon stick for this, also. (See camp potatoes recipe.)

Add pepper and stir until the mixture takes on a dirty brown color. Now stir in the sausage that has cooled, and is in little chunks. (If you cooked patties, chop them up.) Stir in the milk, or half 'n half. Make sure that all is mixed well, and simmers for 5 minutes or so.

Taste and add salt or other spices if you wish. I like to add a touch of hot sauce to mine. This is great over homemade camp biscuits with eggs. Easy to make, and out of this world great tastin'.

Enjoy.

OMELETS ALA NATURAL

Beat 3 eggs together in a plastic bowl. Add 2 Tbs. milk or water, and spices. Just a bit of salt and pepper to start.

Choose a filling for the omelets if you desire. This is a great time to use up leftover chicken, steak, veggies, cheese, you name it! Heat said filling prior to next step, unless the filling is cheese.

Add 1 Tbs. butter or margarine or grease to a hot skillet over medium heat and wait until melted.

Add eggs, and slowly 'tip' the pan on the grill surface just enough to coat the sides of skillet with egg. Egg will cook on bottom and sides of pan.

At this point, add any filling you might want, to the eggs. Add filling to one side of the pan, so 1/2 of eggs is covered, 1/2 is not.

With a spatula, gently lift the uncovered egg away from the side of the pan, and fold it over on top of the filling. Wait for egg to finish cooking, remove from pan (it should just slide out onto a plate).

I've always been partial to salsa on my omelets.

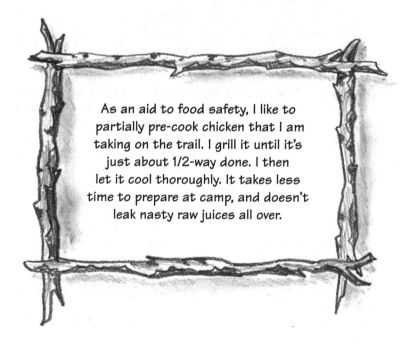

As an aid to food safety, I like to partially pre-cook chicken that I am taking on the trail. I grill it until it's just about 1/2-way done. I then let it cool thoroughly. It takes less time to prepare at camp, and doesn't leak nasty raw juices all over.

BREAKFAST CALZONES

Serves 4

This is an exceptionally simple recipe that brought a round of applause, on a recent canoe trip down the Namekogan River in Northwest Wisconsin.

The nicest part, is they are (can be) prepared ahead of time and reheated on the trip. A snazzy, easy river breakfast! And, perhaps the best part, the limit to the number of different fillings, is as endless as your imagination.

Here's the recipe for breakfast Calzones.

2	Rolls 'pop-open'-type French loaf dough (in refrigerated section of grocery)
8	large fresh eggs
1	large onion, peeled, diced
8	oz. cooked bacon bits, burger, or diced ham or sausage (browned)
1/4	cup green pepper-diced (optional)
1/4	cup button mushrooms (diced)
8	oz. shredded mild cheddar cheese

Begin by cooking meat until browned or near done, add veggies and cook to desired softness. Add 6 of the eggs to the meat, and cook as you would scrambled eggs. At this time, you can season the mixture as suits you. Perhaps a bit of garlic, pepper, and salt would do. Or feel free to add a touch of hot sauce, or salsa for a kick. Remove from heat, and let stand, to cool for 15 min. or so. Drain or pat off any grease.

Sprinkle 1/2 cup flour on a flat, clean surface. Remove dough from package, according to directions. Lay dough on floured area and look for the seam in dough. It should be running lengthwise.

Begin peeling at the seam, unrolling the dough into a flat sheet. When this is done, stretch dough out, so it is as square as possible. With a knife, carefully divide dough into four equal sections, each as square as possible. On each piece, lay about 3 heaping Tbs. of cooked egg mixture, centered.

Upon each pile of egg/meat/vegetable mixture, sprinkle about 2

Tbs. of shredded cheese. Now carefully fold the dough once, corner to corner. Gently pat down the bulge of contents. Using the tines of a fork, press the loose edges of the dough down.

The appearance of the calzone now should be a plump triangular pastry.

In a small bowl, crack in 1 of the eggs whole (yolk and white) and with the second; put in only the egg white

Add milk and whip briefly. Using a pastry or basting brush, coat the top surface of each calzone with this egg mixture. This will help the surface brown nicely when baked, and also lend a nice firm texture.

Being careful to support the pastries while lifting, lay them on a greased baking sheet with space so they aren't touching. It is helpful to poke the tops at least once with a fork. The resulting holes let out steam as the inside ingredients heat up. Otherwise, the tops can get a bit soggy.

Put baking sheet into an oven pre-heated to 350°.

Cook for 15-20 minutes, monitoring their last 5 minutes, so they brown to your satisfaction. They are ready to eat now, just sprinkle on a bit of cheese and set out to cool, then refrigerate.

When wrapped in foil and set over a bed of medium hot coals for 5-10 minutes they will re-heat wonderfully for a nice, easy, no hassle breakfast!

Variations I've tried … pizza calzones, roast beef and mashed potato calzones, berry calzones, chicken and wild rice calzones, and Rueben calzones; to name a few.

The possibilities are endless! Have fun with this one!

"What is man without the Beasts? If all the beasts were gone, men would die from a great loneliness of spirit. For whatever happens to the beasts, soon happens to man. All things are connected."

~ *Chief Seattle, Suquamish Indian Tribe* ~

LUNCH IDEAS TO MAKE FRIENDS AND INFLUENCE PEOPLE

Particularly when I'm kayaking on a lazy summer afternoon, the prospect of a nice, light lunch and a cold beer is a great thing.

On the following pages are some of my favorite lunches that are perfect for this type of eating, or that done while hiking, they are delicious, easy, and involve little or no mess.

AWESOME LUNCH BAGELS

1   10 count bag of your favorite bagels (I love the "kitchen sink" kind, with lots of seeds and stuff on 'em.)
1   8 oz. container cream cheese, garden flavored
1-2   carrots, peeled, whole
1   bunch scallions
1   medium cucumber, sliced in thin coins (on a bias is good)
1   head romaine lettuce, the heart section will do nicely
2   roasted red or green peppers, see recipe for roasting

About 5 oz. Italian dressing, mixed with a bit of pepper, garlic powder, and a touch of hot sauce.

Carrots should be shredded, using peeler. This works perfectly, you'll need about 2 cups carrots.

Scallions sliced thinly, as long, as the bagel is wide.

Pull the lettuce into bagel sized pieces, so they lay flat.

Slice peppers about the same size, and let them soak in the dressing mixture a bit.

Slice bagels and dab cream cheese on both the lid and the base (inside).

Lay on a piece or two of lettuce, cucumber, a bit of carrot, and a bit of scallion. Drizzle on a teaspoon, or two of dressing mixture and top with a slice of the roasted peppers. Put the lid on and slice in half – it's big. Enjoy with some chips, and cold slice of dill pickle.

This, my friends, is what a good, light lunch, is all about!

'WHAT THE HELLS' GNOCCI

In the pasta section of your local grocery, you might find a thing called Gnocci. (That's pronounced no'-chee) This is a sort of pasta/dumpling about the size of a whole peanut in the shell. It has a potato base, and is a great thing to bring to camp.

First of all, not a lot of people may be familiar with it, and it tastes great! It's also very easy to prepare, and easy to keep prior to cooking. And it's cheap!

The stuff I like is in a vacuum-sealed plastic bag, in a box. It's less than three bucks for three servings. It boils up in about 5 minutes, and needs only to have a splash of your favorite sauce added for a great dish.

It can also be added to broth, or stock, as instant dumpling soup. It is a wonderful variation in pasta, and I highly recommend you try it! Melt cheese on it! Pour cinnamon-sugar on it, with butter! Mix it with chicken and sauce! Add a bit of Pesto!

Go nuts, it's Gnocci!

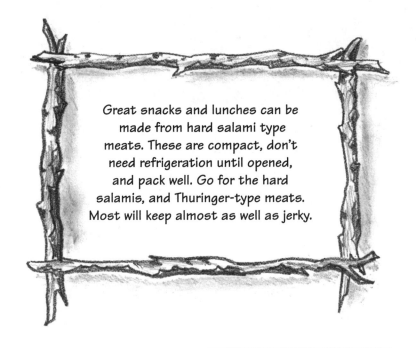

Great snacks and lunches can be made from hard salami type meats. These are compact, don't need refrigeration until opened, and pack well. Go for the hard salamis, and Thuringer-type meats. Most will keep almost as well as jerky.

'RED BANDANNA' KAYAK LUNCH

This is one to remember! It is certainly not a new idea, and is so great partially because of its versatility! Tweak this out however sounds best to fit your tastes. It's a good concept, due to the lack of dishes needing cleaning.

Per person served ... (at least!)

Using an extra coffee cup or other suitable ladle, pour heated chili directly into bag of chips. Pass the ladle to the next person. Holding the bag of warm, delicious chili and chips in one hand, insert spoon with the other. Mix gently. Proceed to eat at your own pace, and smile.

For dish duty, have each person lick off his or her spoon, and put it in their respective shirt pocket for safe keeping. Dispose of the bags responsibly.

"The human mind always
makes progress, but it is a
progress in spirals."

~ **MaDame De Staell** ~

'NOTSO HOTDOGS'

This is a wacky way to cook and I've seen this work well, and I've seen it work moderately well. Kids can do it and thus love their hot dogs even if they are still half cold.

It's really not all that gourmet, but novelty. To a kid, novelty rules!

11 dry 1/2 gallon paper milk carton
1 5x5-inch piece of light tin foil
1 sheet newspaper, crumpled up
1 hot dog (cold)
1 hot dog bun

Insert dog into bun, in the traditional fashion. Wrap in tin foil. You won't want to wrap it real thick. 1 1/2 times around is enough.

Stand carton upright, opening to the top. Insert foil package into carton. Place the piece or two of newspaper around the hot-dog. Paper should fill space, but not too tight or it will not burn.

Light top of carton on fire. Watch, and smile. If all goes well, you will have a warm bun and hot dog at the end of the fire.

I've actually seen this work a lot better using a similar sized and shaped cardboard box. Bon Appetit!

GREAT DIPS MAKE GREAT LUNCHES

Chop into bite size pieces that are easy to scoop with: carrots, green bell peppers, squash, broccoli, cauliflower, tomatoes, green onions, etc. Set out a few dip selections, and maybe some crackers and cheese.

As far as how to make a great dip, some can be store-bought then 'tweaked out'.

Like a jar of blue cheese dressing. Add some crumbled blue cheese, a touch of mustard, and a little garlic. Dip away.

Salsa is a great dipper.

Flavored sour-cream or yogurt is good.

Chip dip is good and as easy as you can get.

Mix a little sour cream with some diced tomatoes, onion, spices, and a can of black beans. Really good!

Guacamole is another wonderful dip as appropriate with chips as it is with veggies; store-bought or homemade. You can really get some good guacamole frozen these days.

These are, for the most, part healthy and easy to prepare. They make for a nice light lunch or snack.

BASIC BUT DELICIOUS BURGERS

1	pound lean ground beef
2	Tbs. steak sauce
1	lightly beaten egg
1/4	cup dry bread crumbs
1	small onion, finely diced
4	fresh buns, or bread
	Assorted toppings, like lettuce, ketchup, pickles,

In a bowl combine the burger, crumbs, onion, egg, and steak sauce. This works best if the ingredients are 'mushed' together well with your hands. For a fun game, you can use one of your hands, and one of someone else's.

Anyway, once mixed well, the burger should be split into four equal parts. Each should weigh about 1/4 lb. Press each serving into a large meatball. Once in a ball shape, flatten it out, by squeezing it between your palms. Rotate it slightly as you flatten, to produce uniformly shaped discs. The discs should be about 1 inch thick.

Prepare the grill, so that you have a medium to hot fire. (You can refer to the 'How hot is Hot' section, for details on heat measurement.) Basically, you want to be able to hold your hand, palm down, slightly above the grill for no more than about 3 seconds before it is very hot. The coals should glow slightly, but be covered with a definite coat of ash that looks like gray flannel.

Carefully lay each burger on the grill where they will receive uniform heat.

After 3-4 minutes give each burger half a spin on the grill. Wait another 1-2 minutes or so, and flip. Wait a minute or two and test for doneness. This is also a good time to lay the buns, insides down, on the grill to heat and brown a tad. Also lay on any cheese that may be desired, to melt.

The more done a burger is, the firmer it will be to the poke of your finger. A well-done burger will appear firm, and solid in the middle, while a medium-rare burger will not be as firm, and will appear softer to the poke. To tell for sure, stick a knife tip into the center of the burger, and look for the desired color meat.

Once they are done to the satisfaction of the guests (don't assume … people like their meat THEIR way) lay each out on the buns in the traditional manner and add toppings as desired.

This is the most basic recipe. You could add crushed garlic, teriyaki, Worcestershire sauce, basil, barbecue sauce, or a host of other things to the raw meat.

Tweak them out the way you like them, and have fun.

THE OLD BREAD BOWL IDEA

This classic recipe becomes even more classic when you look at its possible applications in the field. By baking or buying some large buns and making some hot soup, stew, or chili you create a classic, easy combo.

If you haven't done this or aren't familiar with how it's done, here you go.

The buns I'm thinking of are no smaller than 5 inches around, and at least 4 inches high. Slice as you would for a hamburger bun, except move your cut to the top, leaving the base much thicker than the top. Now, using your fingers or a small knife, hollow out the inside of the base, being *careful not to poke* through the bottom, making a bowl of sorts.

Simply fill the 'bowl' with hot stew or chili, and dig in. The tops, if lightly toasted and placed back on top, make a nice lid for presentation.

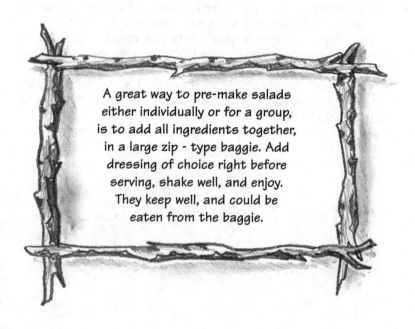

A great way to pre-make salads
either individually or for a group,
is to add all ingredients together,
in a large zip - type baggie. Add
dressing of choice right before
serving, shake well, and enjoy.
They keep well, and could be
eaten from the baggie.

ST. CROIX CHICKEN WINGS

We canoed down the beautiful St. Croix River a few years back on an August weekend that scorched the air, and made the tops of those old aluminum canoes like reflector ovens.

We were lucky to have nights that cooled off nicely, and a good friend of mine that I used to chef with in Minneapolis brought out chicken wings.

Now, there are as many different sauces for wings as there are anything.

This is a nice burner, but has a great rich flavor. Accompanied by a sandy beach, and a few dozen icy beers, these were unforgettable.

> 20 small chicken wings, tips removed. (Just cut through them right at the joint, knuckle down)
> 1/2 cup soy sauce
> 1/4 cup lime juice
> 1/2 cup warm honey (having a warm honey for yourself is just right, too)
> 1/4 cup cracked white pepper
> 6 oz. pilsner beer, flat
> 1 tsp. sugar
> 2 Tbs. cilantro, ground
> 1 Tbs. granulated or minced garlic
> 2 Tbs. hot peppers, minced

You may want to pre-mix the sauce, and cut up the chicken ahead of time. Simply dump the chicken in a Dutch Oven, and bake at about 375° for 20-25 minutes, or grill over the fire for 7-10 minutes. Make sure they get well cooked! Pull apart the largest, thickest one to test for doneness. (See poultry tips)

Once done, slop them around in a big bowl, or pour the sauce into the pot, and mix. Enjoy thoroughly!

If you are grilling these, you may want to wait until the wings are 1-2 minutes from doneness, then brush some sauce on. It will stick to the chicken, and become dry. Give the wings a final toss in the bowl, and chow down.

Omit peppers, for a milder sauce. Perhaps a touch of strawberry jelly stirred into the mix for sweeter, stickier.

Some words of wisdom: "As we let our own light shine, we unconsciously give other people permission to do the same. As we are liberated from our own fear, our presence automatically liberates others."

~ *Nelson Mandela* ~

FAMOUS CAMP DINNERS
I HAVE KNOWN

Grilling Steaks, Venison and Chicken

Grilling can be a lot of fun, if one approaches it correctly.

You have high heat coming from the bottom, and by laying meat directly over it, the meat will cook rather quickly. The trick is in getting it to cook evenly, so the outside isn't burned while the inside is undercooked.

Excessive flipping of the meat isn't necessary, either. Approach the temperature from a 'start smaller, get bigger' attitude.

Very lean meats will dry out if cooked too slowly, though. This is where a good baste or sauce comes in great.

By dabbing on a bit of sauce or marinade, the meat won't dry out as fast.

VENISON ON THE GRILL

Venison is one of my favorite meats to prepare, to cook, and also to eat. I have hunted venison in Wisconsin, Minnesota, and South Dakota.

There are several factors that may make one deer taste different from another. Some of these are age, what it fed on, and whether or not the deer was killed immediately, or ran injured.

If you ask anyone from the Dakotas, they'll quickly tell you that a corn/prairie deer is the best for tenderness, flavor, and size. The endless tall grass, alfalfa and corn, and other native field plants provide you with a deer that may taste very different from a deer raised in, for example, Minnesota's Iron Range. These deer are forest feeders, and rely more on leaves, grass, and bark to sustain them.

One of the most common problems with people who profess not to like venison, is simply that they have never had it prepared correctly.

For more details on how to properly handle deer meat from before it is shot until it is served, see the 'Wild Game' section of this book.

It is my contention that 95% of deer that people say tastes 'gamey' is due to mishandling. I say this because my family and myself are very particular about this and have NEVER had a deer taste 'gamey.' EVER.

I do see, however, other hunters waiting too long before field dressing, leaving the deer to dry out, and chasing them down with pickups before shooting. The latter of which is not only ignorant and unsportsmanlike, but also very, very illegal.

Anyway, onto the recipe, I will sermonize later.

Since venison has almost no fat content, as it cooks, it will dry out. The best way to have deer cooked is between medium-rare and medium. Once the meat gets past the point of medium, it very rapidly dries out, and is more suited to stew or chili.

Often, in the dead of winter, if I am cooking for myself, I may pull out a pack of thin chops to pan fry. Fried in a smear of butter, and cooked quickly on high heat, they turn out great with little more than simple salt and pepper. A quick, no fuss lunch, this is. Maybe slap a couple pieces of homemade bread around it, and it's a great venison sandwich.

But, when taking venison a bit more seriously, I love the heat, smoke and taste that you gain from using an open campfire. Truthfully, there isn't any dish in the world that could be cooked better than on an open fire, as far as I'm concerned.

GRILLED VENISON STEAKS

Quite easy. Start with steaks 3/4 to one inch thick. When cutting meat for steaks and the like, cut against the grain of the meat. (Really, the only time you will cut with the grain is in making strips for jerky.) They should be about 7-9 ounces each. Rub each side with a bit of oil, or butter.

Lay the grill across, a bit less than 1 foot above hot coals. These coals have a thin layer of gray on them, and the only fire dances just above the coals, not higher.

By running your hand just above (1-2 inches) the cooking surface, you should feel quickly that it's 'real hot' there. If your hand can linger, it's not hot enough. If your hand is being licked by flame, or feels like it is blistering instantly, it's too hot.

Lay steaks on, and wait 3 minutes. Give each a half turn, sideways and 2 more minutes. Flip steak over. A nice crosshatch pattern should be on first side. Wait another 3 or so minutes, and add a touch of spice, and plate them up.

The same methods are used for grilling other meats, with the exception being that with beef or pork, for example, you can skip the oil, or butter.

As I've stated before, I like to pre-heat the plates prior to serving, just so they are warm to the touch. This prevents the cool plate stealing heat from the food.

SPLIT WHOLE CHICKEN

A really efficient way to grill whole chickens is by cutting through the ribs (sternum), and then cutting the elbow joints of the wings. This is easily done at home with a set of meat shears or a sharp knife.

If done correctly, the bird can be layed/pressed essentially flat on the grill.

Slowly grill the bottom (inside) of the bird, while applying a splash or two of a white wine and lemon zest marinade. When the bottom is nicely brown and the meat appears to be about 1/2 way cooked or just a touch less, turn the bird over (inside up now).

Slow cook like this, and when ready, turn the bird over once again. The ribcage should be down towards the fire at this point. Ensure doneness either by meat thermometer or by making an incision in the meat. Incision must run all the way to the bone through the thickest meat, usually the breast. When this flesh is pierced the juices should run clear, and the meat should have no pink or red. For more on safe cooking details, see 'General Food Safety and Sanitation.'

Brush on a little BBQ sauce, or sprinkle a bit of fresh herbs and spices.

When removed from grill to plate, this chicken will burst with flavor and can be relished every bite. One of the nicest things about grilling a bird this way is that it greatly reduces the amount of time required to get it grilled to perfection.

POP CAN CHICKEN

This is an awesome method of grilling! And it's very simple in principle and method, to boot! This has gained a lot of popularity with people all over the country. (The birds are still dead set against it for some reason.)

A great variation would be to substitute beer for root beer or cola, as this will lend not only moisture but also a subtle caramel-like taste to the meat.

Simply put, the bird is grilled while sitting upright, rather than laying down. Oh yeah, with a can of soda in its arse.

That's right, take a can of beer or root beer or cola, crack it open and gently insert the can (right side up) into the rear end of the chicken. Some say that talking to the bird in a low soothing voice may help a bit.

Now stand it upright on a medium hot grill that has a lid. Close the lid, and check for progress in about 20-30 minutes. The liquid will boil over a bit, but don't worry. The liquid is moisturizing the meat from the inside, and you will have a fantastic meal.

To finish, carefully remove the can, lay the bird down in the traditional manner and finish searing the bird for a few minutes. Check for doneness (as described in food safety section), and enjoy!

FILET MIGNON en CROUTTE

This dish has become a favorite of many paddlers along the Missouri River and is requested quite often. It's really not too complicated and has impressive results.

Begin by purchasing some good beef tenderloin filets. Ask the butcher for some that are between 4 and 6 ounces each.

Next, in lieu of making your own philo dough, purchase some pop-open-type bread dough. Look for the tube that is designated as French loaf. A regular tube will do, but you will have to stretch and roll it out quite thin before continuing with the recipe.

Prepare a nice medium hot grill (see 'How hot is hot?').

Stretch/roll the dough out on a clean, flat, lightly floured surface. Cut the dough into squares about 4-5 inches across. Lay a piece of dough over each fillet. Loosely stretch the dough so that the 'tails' of the corners are laying under the fillet.

Give the grill a quick spray of oil. Carefully set each fillet on the grill, being sure that the dough 'tails' are still under the meat.

Poke each dough-covered fillet with a fork once or twice. (As the meat cooks and begins to steam, the steam can escape instead of making the crust soggy.) Brush the top of each fillet lightly with a bit of raw egg white. As the dough cooks, the egg will help the crust brown.

Now cover the fillets with a lid, or overturned pot or kettle. I like to set a few hot coals on top of the lid to aid in browning the crust as well as cooking the meat by increasing the internal temperature under the lid.

After about 10 minutes, lift the lid and check. Cook to desired doneness and serve.

If you wish to prepare a nice easy sauce, mix 2 cups water with beef stock, season with garlic powder and pepper, and simmer. Spoon the sauce onto a warm plate, lay the fillet down, and enjoy.

As a nice side, I cut a slab (1 inch thick) of yellow onion, oil well, and grill at the same time as the steak. The onion mellows with the heat and is nicely finished with a touch of lemon juice.

BEEF OR VENISON TENDERLOIN ROULADE: BROKEN ARROW VENISON ROULADE

Don't let the name be intimidating! This is a favorite dish, relatively easy to prepare, with a little patience. And it is worthy of a very special meal, and the bottle of soft, velvety Merlot you've had tucked away, to be shared with the closest of friends and family.

I have prepared this meal with venison tenderloin, as well as with beef and elk. All were worthy of not only great pride, but also once even a few pictures when done!

When I first met Trudi, she introduced me to a unique challenge. (Well, more than one, to tell the truth, but that's another book!)

Anyway, her house had only a wood-burning furnace for heat, and no stovetop, or oven. The house had only recently been equipped with running water.

Well, wanting to make her a really special dinner (because that's the kind of person she is, really special) I accepted the challenge.

I let the furnace/stove run to just coals, inserted my little camp grill (12x18), and laid out this feast. Complete with fire-roasted fresh morel mushrooms and red peppers, it was quite a sight. And one of the best tasting dishes I've EVER had.

I do hope you will try this dish, it comes with my highest recommendations. (And Trudi's.)

Serves 5-6

Tenderloin Preparation
2 1/2 #s of tenderloin strip

Trim off all of the silver membrane on the outside of meat. Use a sharp fillet knife to do this. Cut into one end of the tenderloin, just past the silver. Turn the blade parallel to the silver. Grasping the silver with finger and thumb, CAREFULLY slice toward opposite end of loin. Very little meat should be removed during this process. Also remove any other visible gristle or fat. This meat is as close to perfect as possible.

There are two approaches to stuffing the meat.

One begins by poking a hole through the meat the long way with the knife. Use a long fillet knife and impale the tenderloin from one end all the way through. (Be very careful with your fingers!) Then withdraw knife, and bore a tunnel out a bit with your fingers to make room for stuffing inside.

The other method is to butterfly each loin, being careful not to cut all the way through. Pound out the meat to a thickness of 1/2 to 1/4-inch. You may use a rolling pin, wine bottle, or any other suitable tool. Brush lightly with olive oil, set aside.

Making the stuffing:

1 1/2	**pound spinach, blanched**
2	**egg yolks**
11	**oz. shredded cheddar**
1	**cup mixed mushrooms –**
	shittake, morel, and button work great
6	**thick slices wheat bread**
3	**Tbs. minced garlic**
1/4	**cup minced yellow onion**
1	**Tbs. olive oil**

In sauté pan on med. heat (or over med. coals, cast iron skillet), combine oil, finely sliced mushrooms, and onion, cook until soft. Remove from heat. Mince well the drained, blanched spinach; add to pan. Chop bread into stuffing-like cubes, about 1/2 inch on a side. Add to mixture. Add cheese, egg yolks, and garlic. Stir well, using your hands to work together.

Depending on your approach, either stuff the dressing into the hole from each end until meat can hold no more, or ... if you've chosen the roll-up method; lay meat out flat, and spread filling over the meat in a layer about 3/4-inch thick. Try to leave a small border around edge uncovered. Here's the trick! Going the long way, roll the meat and filling up like a big jellyroll. If you have trouble keeping it rolled (and you will) use a couple pieces of butchers twine, or string to tie it up.

Now to cooking your feast:

Return pan to high heat. Once very hot, stand roll up in the pan, thus searing the blunt, open end. Once one end is seared, turn it over and repeat. Obviously, the roll won't stand by itself, so you'll have to hold it. It won't take long.

Once complete, lay the roll either in the pan or on a hot grill to begin browning around roll. Roll it along, so it browns evenly. Once browned on the outside, put it in either a 425° oven for 10-12 minutes, or cover on grill, and cook same.

REMEMBER: **Venison is best-served medium rare to medium**. (If meat is brown, all the way through, it is overcooked and is really only suitable as stew meat.) This won't take long to finish! The chemical makeup of meats like venison is different than beef.

The meat is cooked to safety, and optimum flavor, texture, and juiciness, when it is **pink in the middle**, and can be eaten even a touch rarer.

Remove from heat and remove string, if you used any. The tenderloin may be served on a platter, whole or plated up after slicing.

If plating, cut medium thickness slices. (about 3/4 to 1-inch thick) Lay on a warm plate and top with another slice, somewhat overlapping.

A wonderful garnish might be sautéed onions, sautéed morel mushrooms, or roasted red peppers. You could make a sauce of beef stock, water, and a touch of cornstarch to drizzle over meat.

Another option that is fabulous, is to take some heated Alfredo sauce and add some black and red pepper seasoning (often sold as 'Montreal' seasoning) and a little extra garlic. Serve the meat over a bed of this sauce – phenomenal!

HUGHES COUNTY PHEASANT SALTUMBUCA WITH CORN POLENTA

The prairie grassland around Pierre, South Dakota is known for many great things, only one of which are some of the biggest, prettiest, and most plentiful (generally) ring-necked pheasants around.

The native splendor of this rich National Grassland is truly inspiring. Hunting these majestic birds is only more of a treat when the cool breeze and the whisper of the corn and prairie grasses welcomes you back to Dakota.

And to top it off, some of the prettiest sunsets that God ever made are found here, over the prairies and the Missouri River Valley.

This unmatched beauty and the magnificence of these wild birds calls for a special pheasant recipe. And, given Dakotas' plentiful corn, here's a recipe for Polenta, (another name for seasoned cornmeal,) which makes a great side dish!

Let's begin by getting our ingredients together:

6	pheasant breasts
30	sage leaves
8	Tbs. butter, or margarine
15	slices Prosciutto ham, or
15	slices thin sliced ham-smoked, or
30	short strips bacon, half-way cooked
1 1/2	cups dry white table wine
1-2	Tbs. Capers, blotted dry
1/2	cup white flour
1/4	cup lemon juice

Begin by cutting each of the breasts into 5 equal pieces. Lay them on a flat, sturdy surface, and pound them out to an approximate thickness of 1/2-inch. For this you can use either a meat hammer, bottle, or rolling pin.

Spray one side of each medallion with a non-stick cooking spray, and place one sage leaf on each, followed by 1/2 slice of the ham, or 2 slices of the bacon. Lightly coat each of the medallions with the flour, until well covered.

In either a non-stick skillet (if at home) or a well-seasoned cast iron skillet, if in the field, over medium high heat, melt 5 Tbs. of butter, or margarine. Place the medallions in the hot butter and cook briefly, to just light brown. Remove from heat, and keep warm.

Return pan to heat, and add the wine, and remaining butter. Let this simmer for a minute or two, until the amount of liquid in pan has steamed away (reduced) by 50%. Add the lemon juice, and the capers. Add just a titch (tsp.) of flour, and stir rapidly until flour disappears, and sauce is smooth. Set aside, and keep warm.

Now let's start the polenta:

1 1/2	cup yellow cornmeal
2	cups heavy whipping cream
3	oz. cream cheese, diced
1/4	cup grated Parmesan cheese
1	Tbs. salt
1	Tbs. granulated garlic
1	Tbs. black pepper

Bring the cream to a slow boil over high heat. Add the rest of polenta ingredients, and whisk constantly. If cream is boiling, and ingredients are whisked quickly, the polenta will be nice and smooth, not lumpy.

On pre-warmed plates, spoon a pile of polenta, and fan out pheasant medallions next to it. Cover medallions with sauce, and add a bit over polenta. Wild rice is also a good accompaniment. Enjoy!

BBQ RIBS

1/2 Rack pork spare ribs, lean
Salt and pepper, and spices to taste
Sauce of choice – barbecue, Cajun, jerk, etc.

Place ribs in a hot oven, say 450° (see heating chart for Dutch Ovens). Braise for a half-hour, turning occasionally, to prevent hot spots. You should have coals over the lid and underneath in a checkerboard manner.

After a half-hour to forty minutes, remove lid, and pull the ribs apart into individual pieces, and add a sauce of your choice. Replace lid, and cook for another 1 1/2 hours to 2 hours over lower heat. For this last bit, 10 underneath and 12-16 on top. (Top ones following the circular pattern, this helps top heat radiate evenly down the walls of the oven.)

You may peek occasionally to check their progress. If the bottom looks as if it may be scorching, add a bit of water or beer. Check for doneness and serve however you like. I like the traditional potato salad and corn on the cob with my ribs.

Tell your guests to use extreme caution if eating these ribs with their hands. The flavor and tenderness of these ribs has excited people into carelessness. It's been known to happen where someone caught up in the moment, bites off their own fingertip, accidentally!

You could marinate these ribs for extra flavor punch. Two to six hours in a marinade of blush wine, garlic powder, red pepper flakes, and a touch of Worcestershire sauce does great. I like to poke the meat many times with a fork, prior to this, it aids in tenderness, and flavor penetration.

THE SON OF BBQ RIBS

Fern's Maple-Mustard Glazed Pork Chops

We were headed for a weekend of turkey hunting in the Black Hills of Western South Dakota when we came upon a sedan parked along the shoulder of the road.

There was an elderly man and his wife leaning over the open trunk, trying to figure out how to get the spare tire and the jack loose to change a flat.

We pulled over, and with the work of two sets of hands, got the tire changed in no time flat.

The elderly couple thanked us profusely and insisted that they pay us cash for our help. We politely refused again and again. Well, they just seemed to want to keep talking. And the man, Sal, kept trying to slip a folded-up twenty into my coat pocket.

Finally, knowing that there was a good diner just up the road, I suggested that they could just treat us to a cup of coffee. They accepted.

When we met at the diner, we shared coffee and talked for a while. What nice folks. The woman's name was Fern and she just loved to talk. I told her that I was writing a cookbook of sorts. Well,

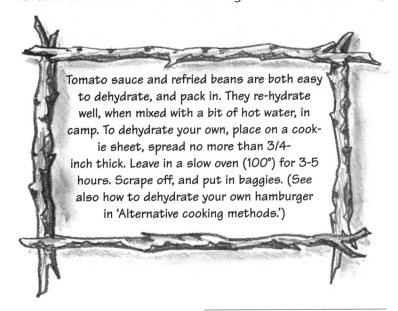

Tomato sauce and refried beans are both easy to dehydrate, and pack in. They re-hydrate well, when mixed with a bit of hot water, in camp. To dehydrate your own, place on a cookie sheet, spread no more than 3/4-inch thick. Leave in a slow oven (100°) for 3-5 hours. Scrape off, and put in baggies. (See also how to dehydrate your own hamburger in 'Alternative cooking methods.')

she about jumped out of her seat. She gave me numerous recipes, scratched out on coffee stained napkins, and asked if I could use any of them. I told her that I would, and that I would send her a copy of the book when it was finished.

This is Fern's BBQ rib recipe. By the way ... they *are excellent*, Fern.

>1/4 **cup maple syrup**
>2 **tsp. cider vinegar**
>3 **Tbs. Dijon mustard**
>1 **shake fresh cracked pepper**
>3 **lbs pork ribs (about 4 pieces)**

Combine above ingredients in a small saucepan and stir over low heat until thickened. Remove from heat.

Arrange ribs on a medium-hot grill. Cover and grill for 20 or so minutes, depending on the thickness of the meat. Flip ribs over and grill for another 15-20 minutes.

About 5 minutes before the ribs are done, remove the cover and brush with the mustard glaze.

Fern said she likes to serve these ribs with either oven roasted acorn squash or sweet potato pie.

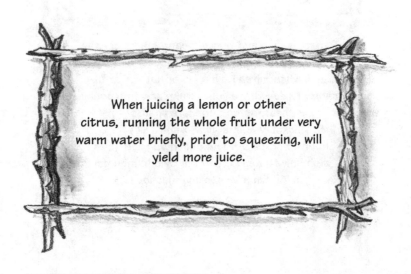

When juicing a lemon or other citrus, running the whole fruit under very warm water briefly, prior to squeezing, will yield more juice.

THE RETURN OF BBQ RIBS

Another favorite recipe from the almighty grill master guru himself, Steve Huff. This guy takes his grilling and smoking as seriously as anyone I know, and he's got it *down.*

Lemon BBQ Ribs

Combine the following ingredients in a small pan and simmer for 4-5 minutes and then set them aside to cool.

1	cup ketchup
1/4	cup brown sugar, packed
1	tsp. fresh lemon zest
3	Tbs. fresh lemon juice
1	Tbs. dark molasses
1	tsp. dry mustard
1/4	tsp. fresh cracked black pepper

Then take 1 1/2–2 1/2 lbs. of beef or pork ribs, and lay them flat. They should then be coated or "rubbed" all over with the following:

1/4	cup kosher salt
1/4	cup fresh cracked pepper
1/4	cup paprika
1/4	cup chili powder

Put the rubbed ribs on a medium hot grill for 15-20 minutes. if coals get too hot or flare up from drippings, give them a squirt with a spray bottle of water (set on mist to avoid ashes clouding the food).

Apply sauce with a brush evenly over the ribs and cook an additional 1-3 minutes or just until the sauce begins to lose luster and crust up.

BBQ RIBS RIDES AGAIN

This recipe comes from my friend Steve Huff. He's a helluva attorney and a chef to be reckoned with. Steve-o, I'm glad I have never had to try to out-cook you.

The recipe works well with beef or pork ribs, but Steve likes them better with pork.

6-12 ribs serves 4-8 people.

For the "rub" you will need the following: Equal parts (say 1/2 cup each) of Kosher salt, fresh cracked black pepper, chili powder, and ground paprika.

Additionally, you will need 3-6 bulbs of fresh garlic.

Preheat oven or Dutch Oven to 350°. Lay out ribs on foil (if in Dutch Oven) or on a baking sheet pan. Sprinkle evenly with the rub. Ribs should be coated on top and bottom.

Place bulbs of garlic (whole and untrimmed) around ribs on sheet or in Dutch Oven.

Cook at 350° 45-60 minutes, depending on the cooking medium and your preference for doneness.

Cut tops off of bulbs of garlic and squeeze them onto the ribs. The roasted garlic should ooze out like paste. Smear this all over the ribs and enjoy!

CRAZY HORSE CHISLIC

Picture this: it's a cool weekend in early Fall in the awesome Black Hills of my native South Dakota, one of the greatest places to go and hike. Drive. Camp. Strip down to your birthday suit and swim in the brisk water of Sheridan Lake with a hot, bright campfire shooting up in the mountain night. The darkness is perforated by winking, far away stars that seem close enough to touch.

I was on that lake on a night like that, and we feasted on some of the finest chislic ever tasted by a mere mortal.

Chislic is meat that is cubed and deep-fried. Originally they used goat, now beef is more common.

I brought a bunch of cubed beef roast, and a friend brought cubed venison. His girlfriend had marinated the meat for a day in a blend of White Zinfandel, Worcestershire sauce, minced onion, a half can of cheap beer, a squirt of some good Louisiana-style hot sauce, a few shakes of granulated garlic, and one Bloody Mary. (Don't even ask)

Another guy had a CD of Jerry Jeff Walker's Greatest Hits. Thank God HE came!

We had one very large Dutch Oven, and a huge old cast iron kettle that strongly resembled one a witch might have. (It belonged to my girlfriend's mother. Hmmm ...)

The pots were each filled with about a gallon and a half or better of oil. (**Careful not to overfill.** *Allow for displacement when meat is added.* Overflowing hot oil onto a fire is not ever a good thing unless you need a raging signal fire.)

Peanut oil works great for deep-frying things as it tolerates the high temperature well. Otherwise regular vegetable oil will work fine. Each cooler of ice-cold beer was spaced so that there was easy access from anywhere around the fire. The kettles were set in the fire on cement blocks, with hot coals and flame all around.

Tasty cold libation was made abundant as we waited for the oil to heat up. You know, because little bubbles start to rise to the top of the oil, faster and faster. The real sign is if you flick in a drop of water, the oil will pop. Careful.

When the oil was ready, we poured in some of each of the meats, which had been well drained of marinade and gave the cubes a few preliminary stirs. The meat cooked fast, and was done to juicy perfection quickly, a nice pink medium-rare. Lifted from the oil with a tin strainer/net type thing, it was allowed to drip and cool for a minute.

Dipping sauces were available, as were cut-up chunks of bread. Another friend had brought out some killer twice-baked potatoes and some awesome 3-layer salad.

I know someone said there were napkins somewhere, but it was so good! I just kept eating. And it was dark. I think I just wiped my hands on my pants mostly, to tell the truth.

We cooked and ate it all, in small batches, throughout the night.

This is a **fun way to cook** on picnics and the like, but when camping, grease disposal is much more of an issue. Plus the kettles are a bit too heavy to carry in by back-pack. We usually had her mom fly them out to us on her broom.

ROCKY MOUNTAIN OYSTERS

I told a buddy of mine that I was including this recipe and he scoffed that it was all just a ploy to whip out a bunch of funny quips about testicles. Like I just have this big bag of smart remarks!

I told him that this was a serious book and vowed that I'd not include even one smart remark.

And, all right, so they're not for everyone.

But for those brave souls out there who have never bitten into a deep fried calf testicle, you don't know what you're missing. (All you know is what the calf is missing.) Anyway, they taste great, and are prefect for any outdoor party or other celebration.

Here's a simple recipe I got out in Sturgis, South Dakota in 1990 during the 50th anniversary of the bike rally. See, this real big biker I know, named Tiny, he walked up to me, handed me a beer and said, "Care for some nuts?"

2	dozen calf or horse testicles
4-5	eggs
4	cups white flour
3	Tbs. each of salt and pepper
1	Tbs. dried Cayenne pepper
1	can evaporated milk
2	cups peanut or vegetable oil

If using frozen testicles, go to next step. If they are fresh, wash them off and remove their outside skin. Then freeze until ready to use. The day of the big ball, partially thaw them, skin them and remove the 'oyster'.

In one bowl, beat together the eggs and the milk. In another mix the dry ingredients, (flour, salt, pepper, and cayenne).

Dip the oysters in the egg wash, then the flour mix and drop carefully into the oil, which has been heated to about 350°-375°.

Cook oysters to a golden brown color, remove from oil, pat dry and serve with crackers, hot mustard, and your favorite sauces. See recipe for 'kickin mustard'.

'!MUOY BIEN' FAJITAS MARGARITA

Cinco de Mayo around a shoreline bonfire ... sounds dangerous to me! It also sounds delicious!

With a bottle of fine Mexican Tequila a few cervesa's, and a healthy batch of these awesome fajitas – you've got a real fiesta!

The first key is the marinade:

1/4	cup fresh cilantro or parsley, chopped
1/4	cup cooking oil
2	pinches fresh shredded lemon or lime peel
1	tsp. chili powder
1/2	tsp. ground Cumin
1	tsp. ground black pepper
1	tsp. minced garlic
2	Tbs. fresh lemon or lime juice (run under hot water before squeezing)

Then comes the meat. Use chicken or beef, or a combination. (I recommend round tip, sirloin, or chuck eye) For chicken: pick boneless skinless breast or thigh cutlets.

If you are using both chicken and beef, split the marinade and use separate containers. Don't use a metal bowl for marinade, as the acid will react with the metal. Plastic, glass, or ceramic bowls are best.

This recipe will marinate 12 ounces of meat total. To make fajitas that are both beef and chicken is awesome. Remember to put them in different containers.

Marinate the meat for 4-6 hours, REFRIGERATED in sealable plastic bags that are sitting in a bowl, in case of leaks. Half way through the marinating time, give each bag a shake, to mix things up.

When ready to cook, prepare grill by providing medium-hot coals. (See also 'How hot is hot' section.) Generally, you will want to be able to lay your hand, palm down, just above the grill surface for no more than about 3 seconds before it is very hot on your skin. The coals should glow slightly, with a nice layer of gray ash over them.

Spray the grill with cooking oil or rub some on with a cloth.

(Don't ever spray over the fire). Lay the meat on the grill, and begin to heat up some soft tortillas. These can just be laid in a stack, in a covered pan over the fire.

After 3 or so minutes, give the meat about half-a-spin. Baste here with the appropriate marinade. I *don't use the chicken marinade as a baste* unless it has been boiled for at least 3 minutes first.

Wait another two minutes then flip the meat over.

Just prior to doneness, lay out a few of the tortillas on the grill. When meat is done (**chicken juices should run clear, and no pink in the middle**) (beef is done to your preference) remove from the grill, and chop roughly into long strips, cutting with the grain of the meat.

Help yourselves to the feast! Common condiments that are almost essential are: Guacamole, chopped lettuce, diced tomatoes and onions, shredded cheddar cheese, sour cream, Pico de Gallo sauce, hot sauce and sliced black olives.

The traditional method is to roll up the meat and toppings in a tortilla shell, and eat vigorously. Often accompanied by copious amounts of Patron' Tequila and traditional Mexican beer. ! Mas Tequila!

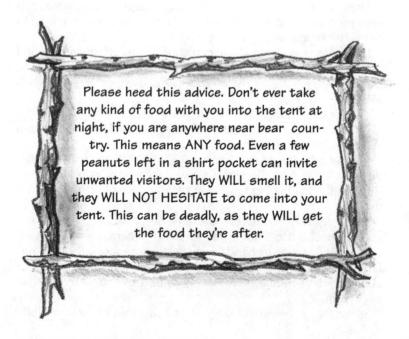

Please heed this advice. Don't ever take any kind of food with you into the tent at night, if you are anywhere near bear country. This means ANY food. Even a few peanuts left in a shirt pocket can invite unwanted visitors. They WILL smell it, and they WILL NOT HESITATE to come into your tent. This can be deadly, as they WILL get the food they're after.

MINNESOTA VENISON CHILI

This is a great recipe that belonged to the Mom of a hunting buddy of mine. It finishes with a great taste!

Here's a great tip for these types of recipes that have a long list of spices. It won't hurt a thing to pack all the spices, pre-measured, together in a container before leaving home.

It is precisely this type of forethought that will serve to make your trips much easier and more enjoyable. Any steps you can take at home to ease the burden on the trail or in camp will be greatly appreciated.

4	lbs. venison (other comparable game such as rabbit, duck, or pheasant) diced (of course ground beef could be used)
5	cups red chili, or black beans (or 1/2 and 1/2)
4	onions, white, or yellow, diced medium
5	hot peppers, jalapenos recommended
1/4	cup vegetable or corn oil
4	Tbs. chili powder
2 1/2	Tbs. cumin
1	dash dried thyme
1	dash dried Oregano
1	Tbs. dried paprika, ground
1	Tbs. black pepper
1	Tbs. ground cayenne pepper
1	large green pepper, diced small
1	Qt. stewed (canned) tomatoes
15	oz. tomato sauce
2	Tbs. granulated garlic
1	15 oz. can of kernel corn

Sauté onions, and peppers until onions are soft. Add the spices, and continue cooking, over medium heat, for another minute or two. Add diced meat, and stir often, so that meat is well browned, but still soft. Add the tomatoes, and sauce, and continue to stir, occasionally. When simmering well, add the beans and their sauces, as well as the corn.

Turn heat to low and let lightly simmer with a loose lid, optimally for 1-2 hours.

Taste, and adjust spices as needed. This, like most soups, will always be better when re-heated, so if you can make this a day or two in advance, all the better.

Nice accompaniments are any of several brands of "chili" beer on the market, and homemade cornbread. (see above recipe)

Of course, you will want to serve sour cream, grated cheddar cheese, and a spicy pepper sauce, such as 'Yucatan sunshine' as toppings. Diced fresh chives and diced red onion will garnish well.

MOMS' CHILI AND CORNBREAD CASSEROLE

This was truly a favorite of mine as I was a child, and still is now that I'm a full grown child.

Prepare chili according to any recipe below, and cornbread according to directions in 'Things on the Side'. Add the chili to a cast iron skillet, about 2" deep; heat, then pour on cornbread batter. Cover and bake at 375° for 20-25 minutes. If desired, add grated cheddar cheese for the last ten minutes of baking.

"YOUR OWN" CHILI RECIPE

Start with a can of any commercial chili and heat. Taste, then add spices to compliment your tastes. Add more burger or beans if desired. Or add a can of corn. Or add a can of another style of beans. Or pull a jar of home canned tomatoes out of the pantry and add them. Or chop and add those leftover chicken breasts from last nights' dinner.

Sometimes, what can be purchased and tweaked to your liking, is faster and easier if you don't have the time or energy and still want to eat well.

ST. PETER DEER CAMPS'
LIVER AND ONIONS – VENISON STYLE

Serves 3 hunters, or 5 non-hunters

1   **FRESH venison liver**
3   **large yellow onions, peeled and sliced thick**
    Spices to taste
    Stick of butter
4   **cups white flour, seasoned with salt and pepper**

This one has become a set tradition with each year's harvest.

I am always careful to gently remove the inner organs and keep them cool and CLEAN when field dressing my deer. As soon as I reach camp, I religiously take the liver right to the sink, and thoroughly rinse it off. Then I soak it in a pan of cold water, and 2-3 Tbs. of salt.

After this, I always make it a point to return to the yard, and take turns carefully relating my days adventures with the other hunters. A somewhat critical ingredient usually accompanies this – a cold beer and a snort of scotch. (*Making damn sure*, of course that all *weapons are safely unloaded* and locked away before making the cocktails.)

This aspect of the day is critical to all the deer camps that I've really enjoyed. It isn't so much the beverage of choice, but the camaraderie of the occasion.

In most camps I've been to it's practically a written rule that a period of time is given to the assembly of hunters and any neighbors that may visit. We all stand out by the hanging, tagged deer. We talk, joke, lie, exaggerate, tease and congratulate each other on the day's hunt. This is done partly out of a true respect for the fallen animals, and is aptly called "visitation".

I think it's also done in appreciation for the safe hunt and recognition of each other for another year we are able to spend together. When a camp ends up short by one or two hunters due to a death or retirement (failing health) of a buddy – it's a sad moment for all. When one is gone, the camp changes forever.

Likewise, it's always a treat to see a new young hunter join the crew, especially if they really are a fit with the feel of things; new excitement, learning and tradition to pass on. And yes, a new target for all of the silly old pranks and jokes that make things like this so fun. (It gets harder and harder to convince the old guys that saran wrap under the toilet seat is truly still funny until they can pull the prank on a greenhorn.)

Anyway, when visitation has been completed (and it isn't truly complete, until each of the party has had an opportunity to relate their brave hunt to the others and chide the others obvious lack of even the most basic hunting skills.) It's time for fresh liver and onions!

Here's how I do mine:

Slice liver into pieces about 1/2 inch thick or a little thicker.

Heat a large skillet over medium heat, then add 1/4 stick of butter. Lay each piece of liver in flour mixture, and coat with flour.

Add floured liver slices to melted steaming butter.

Gently cook liver, until first side is lightly browned.

Turn slices over; add onions, a dash of salt and pepper, and garlic powder. Put a loose lid on pan.

Continue to monitor, giving the skillet a wiggle once in a while, to slide liver around (to prevent sticking) and fry up the onions well.

Liver is done when browned lightly on each side, and is soft but firm to the touch. I think it's best when served medium to medium-well. Internal color should be a light brown, with a mellow line of pink in the middle.

Garlicy skin-on mashed potatoes have become the traditional side dish.

This dish disputes those feelings of dread most of us had about liver and onions, as children. It will become a favorite for many, and is a great way to **pay tribute** to the beautiful animal you've harvested.

Don't forget to bring some rope. Fifty feet should be a good plenty, unless you will need to make several "bear-bags". Also you'll want more if canoeing.
Good nylon rope, as big around as your finger is the best. It has high test, and is affordable. If you are canoeing - again, maybe you'll want to step up a notch.
And it has never hurt anyone to have an extra 50 feet along. Nylon will stretch a lot more than cloth or plastic. The more people in your party, the greater the need for and uses of these items. Always better to have one rope too many than one too few!

J.C.'S BURGUNDY GOOSE WITH RASPBERRY SAUCE

This recipe comes from my brother, Josh who is an awesome chef, a devoted camper, and a good friend.

This is a great recipe for goose, which can be challenging to cook. It sometimes has a tendency to dry out or get chewy. But if cooked properly, like this, it is unbeatable.

For best results, marinate skinned and boned breasts for 12-24 hours in the following marinade:

    1/2 cup cooking oil
    1/4   cup soy sauce
      1 tsp. black pepper, cracked
      1 cup burgundy or red cooking wine

When thoroughly marinated (the goose, not you) brown the goose in the marinade about 10 minutes on each side, using medium high heat.

Raspberry sauce: Slowly bring to a boil the following:

      1 cup raspberry jam or jelly
    1/2 cup water
      2 tsp. brown mustard
      2 tsp. soy sauce
      1 Tbs. Worcestershire sauce
        Salt to taste, if desired

Lay goose on a warm serving platter and cover with the raspberry sauce.

GRANDMA MARY'S DRUNKEN GOOSE

I remember asking my dear Grandma Mary many years ago, "What's the best way to prepare a wild goose?"

She said to place the goose on a wooden cutting board, insert a whole orange into the cavity, sprinkle with salt and pepper and to bake at 350° for two hours, at which time I was to discard goose and stuffing and eat the cutting board.

She has since then come up with a recipe for wild goose that has become a time-honored family tradition. Simple and great tasting-it really keeps the goose moist and tender.

Here, in her words, is the recipe.

Place wild goose breast side down in roaster. Slice and add 1/2 medium onion. Pour 1 can beef consomme and 1 bottle red wine over goose. Cover tightly and cook 5 1/2 hours at 300°.

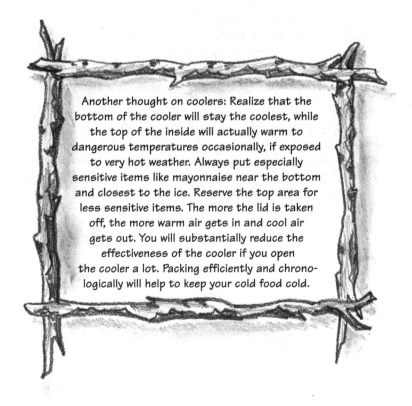

Another thought on coolers: Realize that the bottom of the cooler will stay the coolest, while the top of the inside will actually warm to dangerous temperatures occasionally, if exposed to very hot weather. Always put especially sensitive items like mayonnaise near the bottom and closest to the ice. Reserve the top area for less sensitive items. The more the lid is taken off, the more warm air gets in and cool air gets out. You will substantially reduce the effectiveness of the cooler if you open the cooler a lot. Packing efficiently and chronologically will help to keep your cold food cold.

Odds and Ends –
Some Fish, Game and Turtle Ideas

SUNNIES WITH LEMON
BUTTER AND HERBS

An excellent recipe, with most any panfish. SIMPLE.

2	Tbs. butter or margarine
1/4	cup fine-diced onion
1/2	stalk celery, fine-diced
1 1/2	Tbs. lemon juice
2	fresh lemons
	Salt and pepper
2	Tbs. basil, fresh, fine
1	Tbs. lemon pepper mix
2	cups flour
4	Sunnies, or crappies, cleaned & scaled

Over hot fire, melt butter in pan. Add the onion, and celery, and briefly sauté. Dust the fish fillets with flour that has been seasoned with spices.

Lightly brown the fillets, on both sides. Add the lemon juice to pan and turn fillets over again. (Soaking lemon in warm water will help produce more juice, when squeezed.)

Let simmer for a few (5) minutes and serve. The butter/juice makes a nice sauce. Garnish with lemon slices.

CATFISH PARMESAN – SHORESIDE

Here you go anglers!

4	catfish
4	cups dry breadcrumbs
1 1/2	cups Parmesan cheese, grated
1/4	cup parsley
2	tsp. fresh paprika
1	tsp. oregano
1/2	tsp. fresh basil, fine chopped
4	tsp. salt
1	tsp. pepper

Mix all ingredients well, and use as a breading for your catch.
Place fillets in a hot pan with hot oil or butter. Lightly brown, flip, and brown again.
Serve with rice, pasta or potatoes.

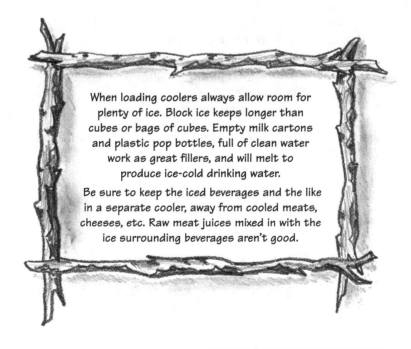

When loading coolers always allow room for plenty of ice. Block ice keeps longer than cubes or bags of cubes. Empty milk cartons and plastic pop bottles, full of clean water work as great fillers, and will melt to produce ice-cold drinking water.

Be sure to keep the iced beverages and the like in a separate cooler, away from cooled meats, cheeses, etc. Raw meat juices mixed in with the ice surrounding beverages aren't good.

CRISPY PAN FRIED RATTLESNAKE

These are seen everywhere in the Dakotas, and as a child I spent many summers on a ranch in south central South Dakota where they were so abundant, it boggles the mind!

My great-uncle Wilbur would spend summer days out in the hay fields along the Missouri River, cutting and raking hay. With every 6-10 passes, he'd have to stop and pull dozens of dead rattlers from the tines of the hay rake.

I brought home many large sets of rattlers cut from these dead snakes, much to my mother's chagrin.

Well, here's a tasty way to cook up these prolific prairie crawlers.

Serves 2

1	lb. fresh rattlesnake fillet, head and skin removed
1/2	cup cornmeal
	Salt and pepper to taste
1/2	tsp. sage
1/2	tsp. parsley
1/4	cup fresh chives, chopped
1/2	cup flour
1/2	cup egg wash (beaten eggs and milk)
	Pinch paprika
	Pinch rosemary, ground

Mix dry ingredients, except flour in a bowl, until well blended. Dip the fillets in the flour, then the egg mixture, and lastly the cornmeal mixture.

In a cast iron skillet, heat oil 1/2" deep. When oil begins to bubble at a rapid pace, lay fillets in oil, using a fork or spatula to avoid splatter burns. When fillets are browned all around remove from oil, and pat dry on a paper towel.

Serve this up on a bun or bread and garnish with scallions, and a dollop of basil mayo or kickin'mustard. (Yellow mustard with hot sauce, garlic, and horseradish to taste.)

May also be eaten on a plate with baked beans, and a light salad. The black bean relish yet to come in this book is excellent with this snake!

BBQ RATTLER

Another way to cook up these lean and tasty things is to marinate them in a barbeque sauce for 2-3 hours prior to cooking. Wrap them in foil, and grill over medium heat.

After twenty minutes or so, begin to baste them with clean, fresh barbeque sauce every ten to twelve minutes – to a total cook time of about 30 minutes.

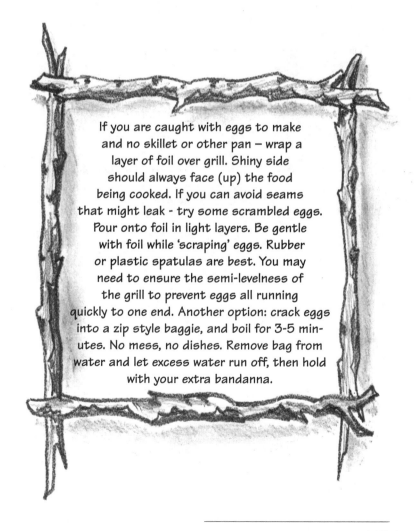

If you are caught with eggs to make and no skillet or other pan – wrap a layer of foil over grill. Shiny side should always face (up) the food being cooked. If you can avoid seams that might leak - try some scrambled eggs. Pour onto foil in light layers. Be gentle with foil while 'scraping' eggs. Rubber or plastic spatulas are best. You may need to ensure the semi-levelness of the grill to prevent eggs all running quickly to one end. Another option: crack eggs into a zip style baggie, and boil for 3-5 minutes. No mess, no dishes. Remove bag from water and let excess water run off, then hold with your extra bandanna.

"One cannot think well, love well, sleep well, if one has not dined well.

~ *Virginia Woolf* ~

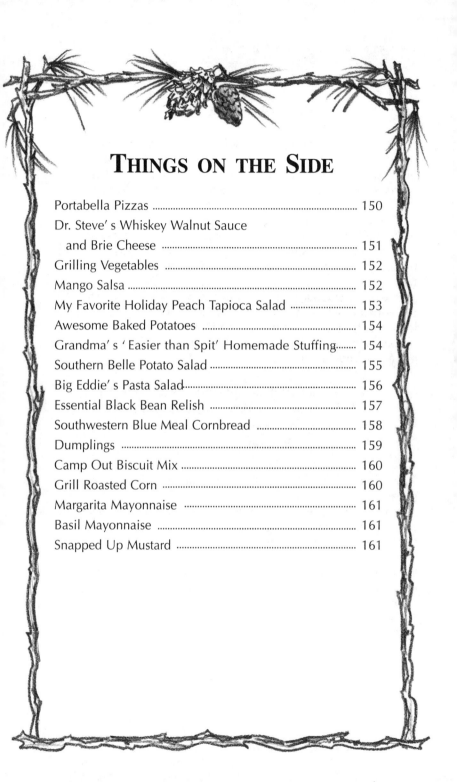

THINGS ON THE SIDE

PORTABELLA PIZZA

This is a favorite along the Missouri River, where I have the pleasure of working as a guide for **Missouri River Expeditions**. We guide guests down the river in kayaks and camp along the shores of regional rivers and lakes of South Dakota, Nebraska, and Wisconsin.

After a day of paddling the scenic and historic Missouri River, we make our landing and treat the guests to dinner, and regale them with campfire discussions of trips past, as well as Lewis and Clark history, astronomy, and other fun topics too numerous to mention.

One of the standards of our dinner menu is an appetizer to whet the appetite before salad, dinner, more dinner, and dessert. What follows is the recipe for one of the favorite appetizers. It is quite simple, and delicious. It also works well in larger quantity as an entrée for vegetarian guests.

> **4-6** **small portabella mushrooms (portabellinis)**
> **1** **jar of good marinara or spaghetti sauce**
> **4-6** **slices provolone or mozzarella cheese**
> **Vegetable spray**

Prepare a medium hot grill. Warm marinara, then remove and set aside.

Remove stems carefully from the portabellas, then gently scoop out enough of the gills to create a 'dish' shape. Spray mushrooms lightly with vegetable spray.

Place mushrooms 'cup side' down on the grill. Grill 5-7 minutes or until tender but firm. Flip mushrooms 'cupside' up. Fill 'cup' with warm marinara sauce, then cover with a slice of cheese.

Cover and grill another 3-4 minutes or until cheese gets soft. Serve.

DR. STEVE'S WHISKEY WALNUT SAUCE WITH BRIE CHEESE

One of the most exciting things that can happen to me is to be presented with the opportunity to collaborate and work with another great cook.

When I started working for **Missouri River Expeditions**, I was introduced to a long-time guide and chef, Steve Feimer.

Now, as legend has it, Steve used to be not only a police officer, but also a Royal Canadian Mountie. Steve is also a certified chef. He now teaches political science at the University of South Dakota.

With a background like that, I knew the guy would either have to be half out of his tree or real, real interesting.

As it turns out, I was right on both counts. Actually – Steve is a great guy, a wonderful chef, and an outdoor nut! I think they'll bury him someday with a saute' pan in one hand and a kayak paddle in the other.

Anyway, I got the pleasure of cooking with Steve a time or two and he gave me permission to include a recipe of his that is a favorite on the river with guides and guests alike. Try this one out for sure – it's awesome!

1/4	cup butter
1	cup lightly packed dark brown sugar
3/4	cup chopped walnuts
1/2	cup pure maple syrup
1	pinch of cinnamon
1/4	cup sipping whiskey (Jack Daniels #7 works well)

Melt butter in a saucepan over medium low heat. Add brown sugar, cinnamon, and maple syrup. Bring to a low boil *stirring constantly*. Reduce heat and simmer for 1-2 minutes or until sugar is dissolved. Stir in whiskey and walnuts.

Serve warm over a triangle of Brie cheese with crackers or slices of baguette bread.

Sauce can be prepared in advance and just heated prior to serving.

GRILLING VEGETABLES

Grilled onions are sweet, and make a healthy, great accompaniment to many meals.

Peel them, and cut in half. Brush with oil or butter, and grill over a slow part of the fire until tender and soft. Try not to turn them much, while cooking, as they may come apart, thus making your job harder.

Roasted or green peppers? Truly a delicacy!

Wash peppers, and coat lightly with oil. Grill whole over a hot fire until the skin is charred and black, evenly around pepper. Remove from heat and cool, perhaps in a pan of cool water, if available.

Once cool; remove skins, they should peel right off easily at your fingertips. Rinse, if desired, and season to your taste. These are also great, cut into slices, and placed in with other ingredients for a cold sandwich the next day. Marinate overnight or for at least a few hours in oil, spices and herbs. (Italian dressing)

MANGO SALSA

This is an awesome accompaniment to fajitas, nachos, and many other foods!

I catered a retirement party on Lewis and Clark Lake last year, and those folks absolutely loved this!

And the simplicity and versatility are unmatched!

1	ripe mango (about 3/4 pound)
1 1/4	cup hot salsa of choice
2	green onions, finely chopped
1/4	cup cilantro, finely chopped

Mix ingredients together and serve. It's that easy. And you should play with this one, substitute peaches, pineapple, etc.

MY FAVORITE HOLIDAY PEACH TAPIOCA SALAD

Grandma Mary made this for the first time decades ago and it is a favorite that has been requested by each child, grandchild, and great-grandchild since then.

2	3 ounce packages peach jello
2	packages vanilla tapioca pudding
1	large can (2 1/2 #) sliced peaches
1	8 ounce carton whipped topping

Drain peaches, reserving juice. Add water to the juice to make 3 cups. Put juice in pan, adding pudding and jello mixes as juice heats. Stir as the mixture comes to a rolling boil. Remove from heat and add drained peaches and cool completely.

Stir in the whipped topping and cool for several hours or overnight before serving.

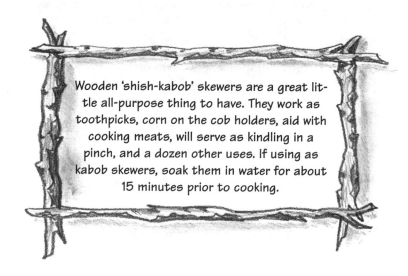

Wooden 'shish-kabob' skewers are a great little all-purpose thing to have. They work as toothpicks, corn on the cob holders, aid with cooking meats, will serve as kindling in a pinch, and a dozen other uses. If using as kabob skewers, soak them in water for about 15 minutes prior to cooking.

AWESOME BAKED POTATOES

Simply wash as many medium to large potatoes as desired. Slice each one, the short way, about 3/4s of the way through, 3 or 4 times.

Peel about half as many onions as there are potatoes. Slice in half lengthwise, then in several slices the wide way.

Insert the onion slices into the potato slits. Rub a touch of butter, either over the potatoes, or actually in the slits prior to inserting onions. Wrap each stuffed potato in foil. Bake in Dutch Oven, at about 400° for an hour, or just above the coals, for an equal time (turning occasionally to prevent scorching).

GRANDMA'S 'EASIER THAN SPIT' HOMEMADE STUFFING

Ol' granny sure had some funny names for things. You should hear Dad's middle name! Anyway ...

If you were thinking you might want some stuffing in your chicken – here you go! Just lay some onions, carrots, and celery around the bird, add a splash of water or apple juice to the pan and cram the dressing into the bird.

2	cups chopped apples, skin on
1/3	cup each of fine diced onion and celery
1/2	Tbs. thyme
1	tsp. granulated garlic
1/2	Tbs. powdered sage (more or less depending on your taste)
1	bay leaf
1	hard roll or bun

Mix all, except the bread, together in a bowl. Push the dressing into the cavity of the bird. As a stopper, push the roll, or bun in last, to hold it all in.

SOUTHERN BELLE POTATO SALAD

There's nothing like good, southern-style potato salad to go with grub on a hot summer day, except maybe an ice-cold bottle of beer, of course.

This is a recipe that has been tried, and tested, with astounding results! It can't be put together in a moments time, but the extra work is well worth it, and nothing goes better with B.B.Q. ribs!

10	large red potatoes, scrubbed
9	eggs, hard boiled, peeled and chopped
1/2	cups mayonnaise
2	large onions, peeled and finely chopped
1	14 oz. jar of sweet pickles (home canned if you got 'em)
1/4	cup apple cider vinegar
1	tsp. salt
3/4	cup yellow mustard
1/2	Tbs. celery seed

Boil the potatoes in a large covered pot or Dutch Oven with salt, until tender. You'll know because skins are soft, and spuds easily poked with a fork. Drain spuds, cool, and chop into cherry-size pieces.

When spuds have cooled and are chopped, pour onions, eggs, celery seed, together with the potatoes, in a large bowl.

Separately blend together the mustard, mayonnaise, and vinegar. Finely chop up the drained pickles, and stir into this mix. Pour this over the spud mixture and gently stir together, until evenly mixed. It's fun to let the kids wash up and mix this together with their hands. They always get a kick out of it.

As with many other things, this is best prepared a day ahead of time and kept well refrigerated. This allows time for all the flavors to meld together a bit. This could be made while at the cabin, or camping and would be great. You could mix the mustard, mayonnaise, etc. ahead of time, and do the rest in camp.

The only concern is for the temperature. The eggs and especially the mayonnaise, demand a well-refrigerated storage area. Keep them well-refrigerated, or in the middle of the ice chest, to prevent any illness from food poisoning. *Store at a temperature comfortably below 40°.*

BIG EDDIE'S PASTA SALAD

Now, I know this is a long recipe, but it's worth it! Ed makes this stuff up at home, then packs it into paper milk cartons, folds the lids over, and duct tapes them. They keep well in a cooler that way. This salad is one of my very favorites!

16	oz. macaroni pasta. Cook, drain and cool.
1	cup celery, diced fine
1	cup red onion, fine diced
1	cup yellow or white onion, fine diced
1	cup cheddar cheese, small cubes
1	cup Swiss cheese, small cubes
1/2	cup Parmesan cheese, grated
1	cup dill pickles, diced
1	cup salami, diced
6	ounces pitted black olives, sliced
1-2	Tbs. Lawrys seasoning
1-2	Tbs. minced garlic
1/2	tsp. white pepper
1/2	tsp. black pepper
1/2	tsp. cayenne
1/2	tsp. dry mustard
1/2	tsp. celery salt
3	ounces pimentos, rinsed and diced
1 to 1 1/2	cup mayonnaise

In a large mixing bowl combine the following: celery, onion, cheeses, pickles, salami, and olives. Put in refrigerator uncovered for 3-4 hours. Remove. Add spices and seasonings. Stir well. Add pasta and mayonnaise. Mix well and cool overnight before serving.
Bon' Appetit!

ESSENTIAL BLACK BEAN RELISH

This easy to make concoction is simply awesome as an accompaniment in tacos or burritos, or as a topping on sandwiches or as nachos. I have made vegetarian sandwiches and hoagies with this mixture as a main filler, just add sprouts, lettuce, diced tomatoes, and cheese if desired.

Just about any way you eat them, this recipe is great!

1	cup diced onion
1	cup fine-diced celery
3/4	cup carrots, shredded or fine chopped
3	12 oz. cans black beans in juice
1	cup ham, diced
3/4	cup cilantro
1/2	Tbs. salt
5	Tbs. hot salsa, or 2 jabanero peppers (fine chopped)
7	Jalapeno peppers, fine diced

In a stockpot or Dutch oven-style pan, cook celery, carrots, garlic, and peppers, in the butter, over medium heat until tender, and slightly translucent.

Drain juice from 1 of the cans of beans, then add all beans to pan. Add cilantro, ham, and salt. Stir, and bring to a simmer. Reduce heat, stir again, and simmer, with lid on, for another 10-15 minutes, stirring occasionally.

It's that simple, and really delicious. And healthy too!

For another great accompaniment, see the recipe for Mango Salsa!!

SOUTHWESTERN-STYLE BLUE MEAL CORNBREAD

The key to this breads success, according to my mother and her mother (from whom this and the next recipe comes), is the hot oil in the bottom of the pan, before adding batter.

1	cup blue cornmeal
1	cup all purpose white flour
4	Tbs. veg. oil
2 1/2	Tbs. white sugar
1/2	tsp. salt
1	tsp. baking soda
1	tsp. baking powder
1/3	cup unsalted butter, soft
1	egg
1 3/4	cups milk, room temp. (Buttermilk is best.)

Preheat oven to 350°. (Or prepare vigorous fire with lots of coals).

Spread the oil around pan (9"x15") or Dutch Oven. Place over heat or on burner, to heat.

Mix together the cornmeal, flour, sugar, salt, and baking powder.

In a separate bowl, mix butter, egg, and milk. Slowly pour the wet ingredients into the dry, stirring well, but not too fast. Mix well.

By now the pan with oil should be very hot, but not smoking, pour in the batter and bake in conventional oven about 30 minutes or cover and bake in Dutch Oven.

If using Dutch Oven method, see baking instructions given earlier in the book. Appearance should be lightly browned on top and springy when done

***Finely diced jalapeno peppers added to the batter add a spicy edge to this awesome bread.

DUMPLINGS FOR CAMP

This is the easiest recipe I know, and is real easy for camp. It's certainly an awesome addition to stews and camp casseroles.

3	tsp. baking powder
1	cup flour
1	egg, whole (less the shell)
6	Tbs. cold water (measure carefully)
1	Tbs. veg oil
1	tsp. salt
1/2	tsp. ground pepper

Beat water and egg together. Add the salt, then the oil, mixing well.

In a separate container, mix together the flour, and baking powder. Mix these into the egg/water mixture well, forming a batter. Drop this, by the spoonful, into boiling stew or gravy.

Cover and let cook for 15-20 minutes.

Done when poofy and browned, but you won't know, since you can't peek, lest a cold breeze blow in, killing their attempt to rise.

I usually mix the dry ingredients prior to leaving, for ease.

These also make an easy dessert, boiled in water and covered with jam, or syrup, or honey. Even melting a slice of cheese over them makes a nice, cheesy, gooey snack on a rainy river day.

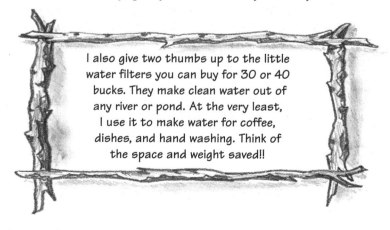

I also give two thumbs up to the little water filters you can buy for 30 or 40 bucks. They make clean water out of any river or pond. At the very least, I use it to make water for coffee, dishes, and hand washing. Think of the space and weight saved!!

CAMPOUT BISCUIT MIX

1/2 Tbs. salt
1 Tbs. white or brown sugar
1 Tbs. baking powder
2 Tbs. dehydrated milk powder
1/2 cup vegetable shortening, or Crisco

Mix the dry ingredients together well. Using two knives, "cut" in the shortening, until all the shortening is in small crumb size. Put into a plastic zip-lock baggie until ready for use.

When ready to use, add 1/4 cup water per cup of dough mix, stir well, and bake as desired.

GRILL ROASTED CORN ON THE COB

This recipe is great for backyard barbequing or for at camp. It's simple and the results are awesome!

Simply soak the ear corn husk, silk and all, in a bucket of clean water for 1/2 hour, prior to cooking. Remove from water and drain excess. Place on a medium hot grill for about 1/2 hour, depending on the size of the ears. Occasionally lift the lid of the grill to rotate corn, so it cooks evenly all the way around.

The outer husks will char, but this is expected. When you want to check for doneness, remove one ear, and peel back a corner of the husk. Squeeze a kernel of corn between your thumb and fingernail. If it pops open and is juicy, the corn's done perfectly. If it is hard to pop and firm – it needs to cook longer. If it is mushy, it's overdone.

Practice this a time or two and you'll see how easy it is to perfect.

Keep some gloves handy for husking and silking the hot corn, as well as a big jar of melted butter for dipping the ears in!

MARGARITA MAYONNAISE

This spread will add zest to any sandwich or salad. I love to grill extra chicken breasts and have them made into cold sandwiches for lunch and add this sauce. It is pretty easy and definitely adds a signature to a sandwich!

About 3	cups mayonnaise, your favorite brand
1/4	cup orange juice, fresh is best
Zest of 2	large oranges
3	Tbs. Gran Marnier liquor
2	Tbs. fresh lime juice
1	Tbs. Gold Tequila

Mix together well and spread over sandwiches or cold meats.

BASIL MAYONNAISE

Transform regular mayo into a real treat by adding a few table-spoons of freshly chopped basil and a splash of lemon juice. Try this on a BLT!

SNAPPED UP MUSTARD

For a great mustard that will delight and surprise guests add to regular yellow mustard: a splash of hot sauce, a dash of brown or stone ground mustard, a sprinkle of granulated garlic. I'm not one for horseradish, but it will zest things up a bit.

THINK OF THE POSSIBILITIES ...

Garlic-lime mayo, jalapeno-lime mayo, southwest mayo, bar-beque ketchup, raspberry honey-mustard (jelly, honey, mustard) ... endless possibilities!!!

Another quote from Thoreau,
for all of the river rats out there:
"The best shod, for the most part,
travel with wet feet".

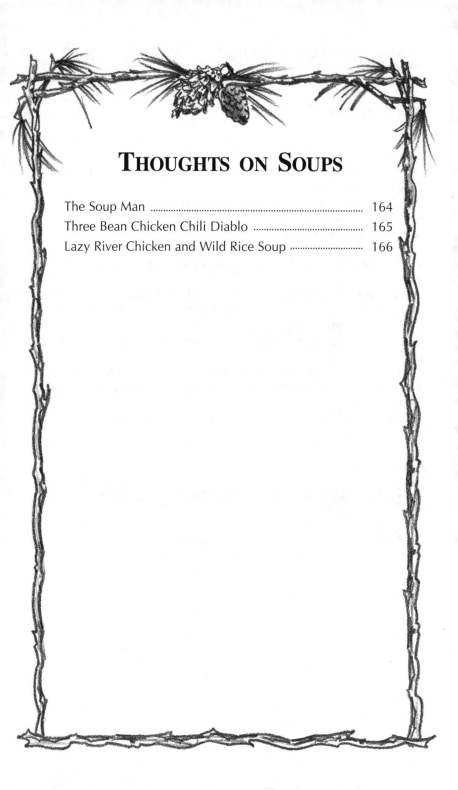

THOUGHTS ON SOUPS

The Soup Man

I have a great fondness for soups and sauces. And if I do say so myself, I've made some dandies over the years.

The problem is that I have seldom, if ever, written down the exact ingredients and processes.

But making a good soup is much like starting a fire, I think. If you have assembled the right ingredients, go with your instinct, and take your time, your chances of success are good.

I chose to include just a couple of my favorite recipes that I have collected from friends and family over the years. Each one is a winner.

It is commonly accepted that soups and most sauces (and a few other things that I won't go into) get better with a bit of age.

You'll notice how any chili or stew seems to get better a day or two after it was first created. The flavors marry and the true essence shines through.

I prepare most soups ahead of time, and re-heat on the trail or camping. It makes an easy, no-fuss meal, and is always warming and delicious.

Enjoy these few soup recipes and tweak them out your way.

Speaking of bears, if you are in bear country, you may want to forgo the citronella bug spray. It has been said that some bears are attracted to the smell of citronella. And it is easier, after all, to swat mosquitoes than bears.

TRES FRIJOLES POLLO CHILI DIABLO (THREE BEAN CHICKEN CHILI-HOT)

I made this for deer camp last year and it was great! No muss, no fuss, easy and great.

6	grilled boneless, skinless chicken breasts, chopped
1	quart cooked white beans in sauce
1	can red beans, cooked, in sauce
1	can black beans, cooked, in sauce
1	large yellow onion, diced
1/4	cup diced peppers; jalapeno (optional)
2	pints salsa or picante sauce
2	cans kernel corn, drained
	Spices to your taste; cumin, oregano, salt, garlic, chili powder
	Habernero or jalapeno pepper sauce (optional)

Combine ingredients in pan. Heat and let simmer. Serve hot with tortillas and cold beer.

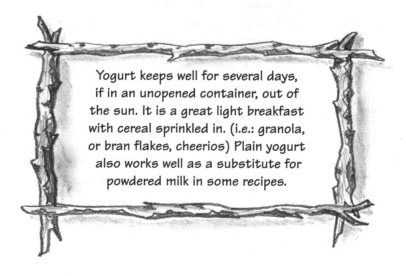

Yogurt keeps well for several days, if in an unopened container, out of the sun. It is a great light breakfast with cereal sprinkled in. (i.e.: granola, or bran flakes, cheerios) Plain yogurt also works well as a substitute for powdered milk in some recipes.

LAZY RIVER CHICKEN WILD RICE SOUP

Of all the recipes I've tried for this over the years, this one is the best! I always include this on the menu when we are out in the fall or winter months. The flavor and richness are very satisfying.

I always make my soup in big batches, especially this one, it won't last long!

This process involves making a roux to thicken the soup, it is certainly not complicated.

ROUX:

18	ounces butter
3	cups flour
1	minced yellow onion

SOUP:

3	cups uncooked wild rice
3	quarts chicken broth (4-5 oz. chicken base and water)
1 1/2	quarts half and half
3	tsp. salt
2	cups minced ham
4-6	cups chopped cooked chicken (skinned and deboned)
1	cup slivered almonds, optional

Method: Melt butter in saucepan and briefly saute' onion. Blend in the flour and remove from heat.

In a large stockpot, bring 2 quarts of water to a boil and add the salt. Stir in the two cups wild rice (rinsed). Cook rice until the kernels are tender and open but NOT MUSHY. Drain and set aside.

Boil three quarts of water, add the chicken base and stir well. Bring this stock to a rolling boil. It is very important that the water is at a rapid, rolling boil. Slowly stir in the roux (butter, flour, onion) while stirring constantly. Now pour in the half and half.

Stir in the other ingredients: rice, ham and chicken, almonds.

This is a time tested and wonderful soup that is perfect for camp, or any holiday party, or just to warm up a cold winter night at home.

"A man hath no better thing under
the sun than to eat, and to drink,
and to be merry."

~ *Bible* ~

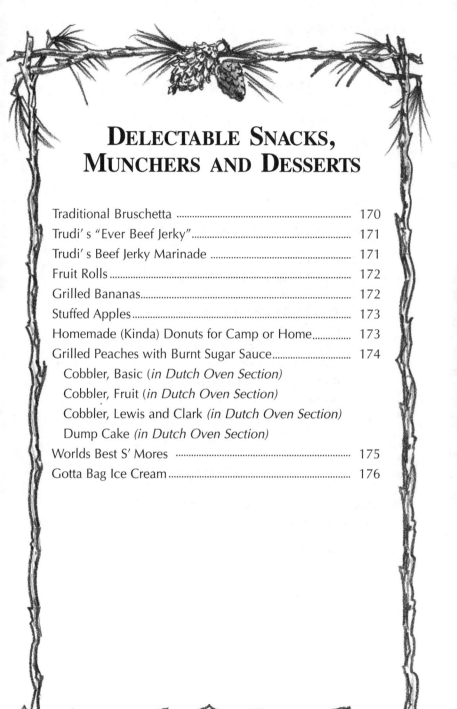

DELECTABLE SNACKS, MUNCHERS AND DESSERTS

TRADITIONAL BRUSCHETTA

This is an excellent, light, healthy appetizer or snack. It is very easy and affordable to prepare. It is a very widely served item in better restaurants, and will prove very pleasing in the outdoors.

Consider your camp dining room the best in 'Al Fresco' dining. Serve this on a hot afternoon as a snack, or with some wine as a romantic appetizer.

A recipe that generously serves 4-5 is as follows.

10	Roma tomatoes. Others may be used, but may be too juicy.
2-3	Tbs. minced garlic
6	Tbs. fresh chopped basil. Go with the fresh stuff here, for sure!
2-3	dashes oregano, salt, and black pepper
2	Tbs. white sugar
1	baguette, or French loaf sliced thin, making 15 or so slices.
1/4	cup grated Parmesan cheese
	Cold butter or margarine

Romas are perfect for this recipe. Otherwise, just drain off excess juice prior to mixing.

Chop the tomatoes well, discarding the stems. They should be finely diced. Drain excess juice if necessary. The consistency should be very moist, not runny.

Add spices, basil, sugar, and garlic. Mix this all together well and set aside to cool, for a half-hour or more.

When tomato mixture has had time to cool and share flavors, lightly butter each slice of bread and lay on a medium hot grill, to toast lightly. Try to insure that it gets somewhat crisp, but not dry, like a crouton. When toasted, add a dollop of tomato mix on each slice of bread, covering the toasted, buttered side.

Add a pinch of grated cheese to each, and serve.

TRUDI'S "EVER" BEEF JERKY

This recipe is quickly becoming legend in northern Wisconsin. Perfect for any activity, it stuffs into any shirt pocket, needs no refrigeration, and although it's chewy, it's not tough. Ever.

The only drawback is that even though we dang near double our recipe every time, we never have enough. Ever.

Follow her directions here, and you'll never want to canoe, hunt, or camp without it again. Ever.

The only danger here is that you should take every precaution to make sure your dogs never get so much as a sliver of it, even by accident. If this happens, the dogs will be instantly begging for more, barking and drooling and dancing all over until they get more.

Come to think of it, I've seen people react just the same!

Ask your butcher to cut some top round steak into strips for jerky. Combine the following ingredients and soak the beef, covered, at least four hours, preferably 6-8 hours, in the refrigerator.

Drain the meat of excess marinade. Lay the strips out on dehydrator racks, according to the dehydrators instructions. Dry until the jerky sort of cracks when you bend it.

If it gets too dry it will be hard and unpleasant to chew. If it's under-dried it will be too soft and still may spoil and make you sick.

Trudi's jerky is always just right and tastes great.

TRUDI'S BEEF JERKY MARINADE

1 1/2	pounds beef
1	cup soy sauce
1	Tbs. garlic powder
5	splashes Worcestershire sauce
1	tsp. dry mustard
1	tsp. black pepper
1	tsp. celery salt

Add water to marinade until all meat is covered in liquid.

FRUIT ROLLS

1	container pop-open dough, 'french loaf'
1/4	cup soft butter or margarine
4	Tbs. cinnamon sugar
1 can,	peach or berry pie filling (or drained
or 3 cups,	peaches, chopped)
1	cup white flour

Open the dough, and lay on a clean flat surface that has been dusted with flour. Looking for the seam running lengthwise along dough, gently pull apart at seam. Dough will unroll into a sheet about 1 foot square.

Lightly spread a bit of butter on top of dough. This should be just enough to lightly cover dough. Sprinkle with cinnamon sugar. Spoon out fruit filling over dough, evenly. Leave just a small border around outside uncovered.

With a gentle touch, re-roll dough, jelly-roll style. Coat your fingers in a bit of flour to prevent dough from sticking to them. Slice roll into sections, or wheels about 1 1/2 inches thick. Use a knife for this, or use a piece of dental floss or string.

Lay in lightly buttered muffin pan, pie tin, or tin plate.

Bake in Dutch Oven at about 350° for 35-40 minutes.

GRILLED BANANAS, AND FRUIT

Slice through the middle of a banana *from* end to end, but *not through* either end. Grill right in their skins, cut the rest of the way, and spoon out the meat, when soft.

Mmmmmm, I'm telling you, here's the place a case of the munchies meet a beautiful end. Poke in a few chips off a chocolate bar, even better! (A dab of peanut butter?)

STUFFED APPLES

A great, easy recipe, so simple it's widely used it Scout Camps all over.

Simply core out as many large apples as needed (one per serving), but save the end pieces. (Cut away the middle of the cores from the top and bottoms of the core.)

Mix together some cinnamon/sugar and some raisins, and stuff the cores of the apples.

Replace the end pieces of the core, wrap apples in foil, and lay on the coals for 5-10 minutes, turning a few times, to cook evenly. Unwrap and feast on this simple, delicious, and healthy snack! Any leftovers will save well for later, in the cooler.

HOMEMADE (KINDA) DONUTS FOR CAMP OR HOME

These donuts are so easy, and good, you and the kids will just love 'em.

You buy store-made biscuits, the kind in the pop-open tubes.

Heat up oil either on the grill, or stove. A quart or two should do plenty of donuts. Heat the oil, until it's bubbling a lot, and is quite hot.

With each biscuit, poke your finger through the middle, making the hole. Or you can punch out the holes with a film vial, or other suitable utensil. Drop them in the hot oil, let cook until brown on one side, then flip 'em. Remove when done with a spoon, spatula or whatever. (no plastic – duh.)

Set on a paper towel to dry; roll in cinnamon sugar, and enjoy. Careful you don't burn your mouth.

Also, no sense in throwing away the 'donut holes'. Hint, hint.

GRILLED PEACHES AND BURNT SUGAR SAUCE

I brought this recipe home for Thanksgiving a few years ago and it was a hit with my family.

> **1 cup sugar**
> **2 cups heavy cream**
> **1 pinch nutmeg**
> **1 pinch cinnamon**
> **4 large firm peaches; thin skinned,**
>   **pitted and cut in half**
>   **Vegetable spray or vegetable oil**

Heat a thick-bottomed saucepan over medium heat. Add sugar and stir to level in the pan. Cook 5-7 minutes, stirring occasionally to let the sugar brown evenly. Use care not to scorch sugar. Remove from heat when browned.

In a separate pan, carefully bring cream to a simmer. Stir in nutmeg and cinnamon and simmer for 8-10 minutes, then stir in hot sugar and dissolve. Remove from heat and let cool to just warm.

In this time, give each peach half a spray of oil on its inside.

Lay peaches on a medium high grill about 6 inches above the heat. Grill for two minutes, then rotate 1/4 turn and cook for two to three more minutes. Peaches should be warmed through and have sear marks from the grill surface.

Slice each piece in half (now 1/4s) and serve with wedges of angel food or pound cake and drizzle with sugar-cream sauce. Perhaps garnish with sliced or fanned strawberries. It also is accompanied well by a huge scoop of vanilla ice cream.

WORLDS BEST S'MORES

S'mores are many people's favorite campfire treat. And, they definitely cheer up a winter night stuck at home, for the kids. Sometime try that in the oven at home.

There are a few ways you can jazz up the old standard and make it better. Here are a few variations ... Lay the graham cracker out on a hot rock next to the fire, and put the piece of chocolate bar on top. While roasting the marshmallow, the cracker and the chocolate will soften just a bit, thus not crumbling when bitten into. Another way is to incorporate a little peanut butter into the scene, either by using peanut butter itself, or perhaps a chocolate and peanut butter candy cup. You could shortcut by using the little fudge striped chocolate cookies as the outsides, with warm roasted marshmallows inside.

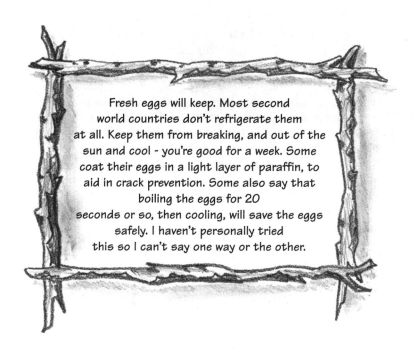

Fresh eggs will keep. Most second world countries don't refrigerate them at all. Keep them from breaking, and out of the sun and cool - you're good for a week. Some coat their eggs in a light layer of paraffin, to aid in crack prevention. Some also say that boiling the eggs for 20 seconds or so, then cooling, will save the eggs safely. I haven't personally tried this so I can't say one way or the other.

GOTTA BAG ICE CREAM

I got this recipe from my brother, who trained as a chef in Minneapolis and is now Executive Chef at a hip little place in downtown Sioux Falls, SD.

He is as avid a camper and cook as one would ever meet. It must be in the genes.

Anyway, this recipe is one of his many contributions to this book and actually works real well. I remember making this for a youth group on a kayak trip down the upper Missouri. It had to be 100° in the shade that evening and we ran out of extra cream to make more ice cream and I thought we had mutiny on our hands! Try this one out and enjoy. It takes patience, but a lot of worthwhile things do.

1	coffee can or other similar circular container
8	cups light cream (half and half)
4	1-gallon size zip-lock baggies
1	cup rock salt
1	vanilla bean (or vanilla extract)
1/2	cup granulated sugar
Approx. 5	lbs. cold ice (as opposed to warm ice?)

Fill each quart bag with 1 cup cream, 1 Tbs. vanilla extract and 2 Tbs. sugar and seal the bag very well. Place the filled and sealed bag in the center of the can or container, and pack ice and 1/4 cup rock salt on all sides.

Now, sit across from a friend and roll the container back and forth for 10-20 minutes until the ice cream thickens properly. Remove the bag from the container and open the seal and enjoy!

DESSERT RECIPES CAN BE FOUND IN THE DUTCH OVEN SECTION OF THE BOOK. COBBLERS, CAKES, AND MORE.

"Everything has its Beauty, but
not everyone sees it."

~ *Confucius* ~

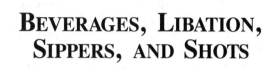

Beverages, Libation, Sippers, and Shots

CAMP COFFEE

This is no French press or latte', by any stretch – but it will get the ol' ticker going again after a chilly night! How much coffee you'll need to take along depends on how much you need to take in each morning.

And it may be nice to offer a cup to a passing hiker or others you may meet, if you're so inclined. This is regarded as being one of the most regal courtesies you can share with passers-by passing by in the woods.

By the way, you won't believe this, but I actually saw someone whip out an expensive little jr. sized electric coffee grinder on a three-day hike one time! A full days hike from the nearest dirt road and ... well, you get the idea.

He filled his grinder with gourmet beans, looked up, cord in hand, saw us looking at him and realized his oversight.

That was the first time I saw a grown man eventually hit the dirt, he was laughing so hard! I have to imagine that little machine got heavier in the pack with each step he took after that. Many peo-

ple carry shiny new gadgets resembling small cappuccino machines, and some make do with an old fashioned 'set on the fire, percolate cowboy style' type pot.

If you've lost your percolator basket, here's a method that will see you through, guaranteed.

Simply take a sock (one without holes, if possible, and a clean one always makes the coffee easier to swallow), roll it downward towards the toe, about half way. Add one tablespoon of coffee grounds, per cup of coffee desired, and one whole egg. Unroll the sock to its full length, and squeeze, breaking the egg. Massage the goop a bit and tie shut or otherwise close the end of the sock. Place the sock in a pot of already boiling water for about 5 minutes, and remove sock.

Pour coffee into favorite camping mug, and enjoy the morning perhaps, with some venison hash. (recipe in breakfast section of book.)

If for some reason you don't have a sock suitable for 'coffeeing', think about using a bandanna.

Another method is just to dump the grounds in the water, bring to a boil, and when ready, add a splash of cold water. This will temporarily settle the majority of the grounds, so you can pour.

Or if you have the basket but no liners, cut a piece of napkin or better yet, paper towel. They work so well you'll think twice about buying liners.

EASY SUN TEA

No reason to go without a splash of tea in the hot summer sun. Hey, it's hot enough to give you an almighty wicked sunburn and make you thirsty, it's hot enough to brew a little tea.

I fill a Nalgene bottle or milk jug with water in the morning, add a few tea bags, and strap it to the deck of my kayak. By afternoon it has brewed and stewed to perfection. Drop in a few ice cubes snuck from the cooler when no one was looking, and I'm ready to drop my feet over the side of the kayak, and sip some fresh tea.

Quite a nice refresher.

HER MAJESTIES LEMONADE

This is a tasty libation for a hot summer day!
I like to use **Beefeater or Bombay** brand gin.

In a tall glass full of ice, pour in 1 1/2 ounces fine gin.
Fill to the top with lemonade, pink seems to work nicely.
Insert straw, swirl twice, remove straw and sit back and relax.

RUM AND SODA CLOUDYS

Another fine sipper! This has become a staple adult beverage on some of our hot summer canoe and kayak trips.
Bacardi Silver Rum is great, but a favorite of ours is Matusalem. (WOW! GOOD!)

Fill a tall glass with freshly chilled ice, and add 1 1/2 ounces rum of choice.
Add 2 or 3 splashes of cola, and fill to the top with soda water. Squeeze the juice of lime wedge into drink, then drop wedge into glass. Insert straw and swirl to mix. Remove straw and place behind ear.
Sit back, relax, and enjoy each others company in the serenity of the great outdoors.

Following the path of least resistance is
what makes rivers and men crooked.

~ Anonymous ~

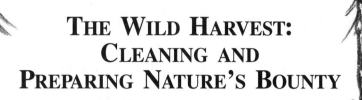

THE WILD HARVEST: CLEANING AND PREPARING NATURE'S BOUNTY

THE WILD HARVEST:
CLEANING AND PREPARING NATURE'S BOUNTY

'PRAISE THE LORD AND PASS THE AMMUNITION'

One Difference Between Hunters and Sportsmen:

When reading the wild game recipes, consider this thought: it really has to be a bad day for me to consider any day hunting "unsuccessful".

I mean, something really major has to happen, for me to say the day was wasted. I've seen hunters and fishermen who, just because they didn't fill their limit, curse their luck in frustration. These guys often have had a whole day or even a week, outdoors with their friends, dogs, or alone.

Regardless of whether or not you fill your tag or possession limit, don't forget to enjoy yourself. Don't forget to notice the intricacies.

In the end, it was a day spent outside in the fresh air. That in itself, at least for me, is quite a catch.

Myths and Realities About Wild Game:

I want to dispel a few myths and share a few pointers.

Compared to domestic meats like pork and beef, game is leaner, richer, and healthier. It contains far fewer of the synthetic chemicals commonly found in domestic animals. It's lower in calories, and fat, and generally higher in protein, and certain minerals, like Thiamin, and Niacin.

But wild game is also generally harder to come by than domestic meats.

And if you're a non-hunter who wants to eat game, there are a whole other set of issues. The market prices are far higher, and restaurant game often isn't truly wild, having been raised on a game farm or ranch.

So it always pays, in my opinion, to use high quality accompanying ingredients, when preparing wild game.

If a recipe calls for **wine**, select a good table wine rather than 'bottom barrel' stocks. No need to use top-shelf rare vintage, by any means, just use decent stuff.

If a **meat stock** is called for, try not to substitute the dry, bouillon-type, opting instead for homemade, or at least the moist, soft varieties available at groceries.

When **fresh herbs** are available, always use them instead of the dried ones. Your recipes will have that extra zest that wild game deserves, and your guests will notice the difference in taste and appearance.

Other variables to certainly consider are the types of game used, and how it has been killed, processed, and stored.

The sex of the animal, the time of year it was killed, and how it was cared for after the kill, will invariably affect the ultimate **quality of the meat**. Most important of these factors, is how it was stored, wrapped, and frozen.

Great pains should be taken to insure that the animal was killed quickly, the carcass field-dressed and cooled promptly, and the meat stored cleanly. The larger the animal, the longer it will take to cool it to a safe temperature. (30-35 degrees is optimal.)

The biggest threats to a game animal, after it's been killed, are time and temperature.

Field Dressing Large Game

I am by no means a professional butcher, nor do I profess to know everything about wild game. But should the opportunity arise that you wish to do some of your own butchering and you have no instruction, here's a basic rundown on large game, using a deer as an example. Rabbits are basically the same, just a hare smaller.

By spreading the ribcage as wide as possible (without breaking ribs), and removing all entrails quickly and carefully, you allow the **cooling down process** to speed up. A common mistake is for the hunter to leave a portion of the windpipe in the neck of the animal. Care should be taken to remove the entire windpipe, as it will hold heat in the neck, and spoilage will occur in this area much faster.

Make sure to cover the animal with a game bag, light bed sheet, or other cloth that will allow the carcass to get air, but keep away flies, dirt, and hot sun; if such are in season.

Some people like to use as much of the animal as possible, and I clearly support this. But, often overlooked by hunters, are the internal organs. Yes, they are good snacks for the dog, but the **heart and liver** are wonderful eating.

Save the heart by removing and cooling it as quickly and thoroughly as possible Run the heart under cool water, massaging to expel as much blood from the inside as possible. Keep it covered and refrigerated until use, in a wet cloth. Boiled until well-done with spices, then cooled, and sliced thin, it makes a wonderful sandwich meat, and tastes a lot like roast. A little mustard, and you're ready to eat!

I also pickle elk and deer hearts, using any of several standard recipes that are available.

Other organs that deserve a try are the kidneys, sweetbreads (mainly the pancreas, a lumpy organ right behind the stomach) and liver, there's a recipe for liver here.

And obviously, don't forget to cut out the backstraps now. They are parallel to the spine, on the inside of the animal. Think of them as smaller tenderloin meat.

Don't transport the animal on the **hood of your car or truck**. Engine heat can ruin the meat. Remember, keep it cool. Hey, you (or somebody) worked awful hard to get the meat this far. (Not to mention the sacrifice the animal has made!)

You may hang the carcass for a few days, at the proper temperature and humidity (optimally between 30-35 degrees). This process of **aging will often enhance the taste** of many different kinds of meats, including elk, moose and venison. If you don't have access to the proper conditions for whole-storage, skin the animal right away, cut it into a few sections, and cool it right away in a cooler or ice chest.

Or take it to a commercial butcher, with the facilities to store and butcher the carcass. They will ask you what types of meat you want and what to process the remainder into (i.e.: jerky, sausage, burger, etc.)

If you opt to do the butchering yourself, there is additional satisfaction. And if you have never done this, fear not ... if you end up with a few odd shaped pieces at the end, well, it's that much more for the 'stew meat' pile!

One hint, on temperature, is that not only will your kill stay preserved better if kept quite cool, but the meat itself will be firmer, and much more easily handled.

Also, if the animal hangs for at least several hours or overnight before being skinned, most fleas and ticks will abandon the cold carcass.

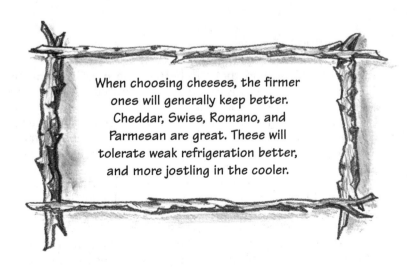

When choosing cheeses, the firmer ones will generally keep better. Cheddar, Swiss, Romano, and Parmesan are great. These will tolerate weak refrigeration better, and more jostling in the cooler.

Skinning

Skinning is pretty elementary. If you've never tried it before, read this section once or twice from start to finish. Start in to work, and look back to the book as needed.

Hanging the animal well supported, tied through the hocks (shin) bones, head down, slice a circle around the hocks 'below' the rope. The cut should only go through the skin.

Once you can put the tip of the blade under the skin, and cut from inside out, (blade up) against the flesh, much less hair will be on the meat. Also, cutting through the hair dulls an edge quickly. Make an incision from the initial ring down the 'front' of the thigh as far as the hips. Peel each leg skin down to the butt. Peel by grasping the hide firmly and pull steady but slow.

Cut appropriately to clear the anus, and the butt area. You will need to cut through the tail cartilage. Once beyond this, the proper way to continue pulling the skin off is as follows. Work in small 'pulls', going only a few inches at a time, until you get the feel of it.

Grab a fist full of skin and fur, and roll it up, in your right hand. Place your left forearm on your right wrist area, horizontally. Lean your body weight on this. Pull as evenly as possible. This method will shed little hair. Pull down to the 'head' end of the neck, and cut hide to remove.

Butchering

Let's keep in mind that the best of the meat is along the spine. On the back (out)side running parallel to the spine are two long strips called the tenderloins.

On the inside (gutside), running along the same way as the tenderloins are the backstraps. They will look like the tenderloin only smaller and skinnier. These should have been removed when field dressing the deer to prevent drying out.

As you prepare to split the deer in two, be very careful not to damage this meat. I personally do the removal of these pieces first.

Let's start at the point, where the deer has been skinned, and is hanging by its hocks, on a crossbeam.

There are two approaches to butchering from here out. One is to cut the deer laterally down the spine and proceed, the other is my preferred method. I will discuss the lateral method first, then the other method. You pick.

Lateral Method: Stand facing the rib-cavity. The spinal column of the deer should be easy to see.

Move to the backside of the deer, away from the rib-cavity. Cut a slit from pelvis to nape, running **DIRECTLY over the center of the spine**. This will give you a 'sighting line' to follow with your saw, and reduce the amount of meat you have to cut through with the saw.

Move back to the cavity side of the deer, and begin sawing at the crotch straight down the spine, towards the ground. The goal here is to split the carcass into two lateral halves. At that point, remove one half from the hanger, and lay it on a clean surface. This, ideally, would be stainless steel, but since that isn't always available, cover a clean table with butcher's paper, shiny side up.

Now, the removal of the front quarter should be easy. Cut around the shoulder, under the arm and lift it away from the

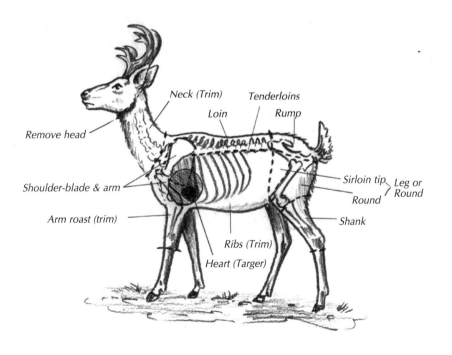

191

ribcage. I generally prefer to use this meat for stew meat, and the like. Some like to roll it into roasts, but to each his own.

The hindquarter will be removed by cutting just in front of the 'pin bone', following it around, and then sawing through the bone. Now the choice is to divvy up the meat between roasts, chops, and steaks. With the hindquarters, I prefer to separate the muscles at their natural divisions, yielding several nice smaller roasts.

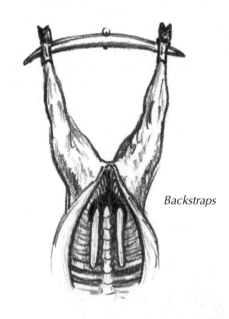

Backstraps

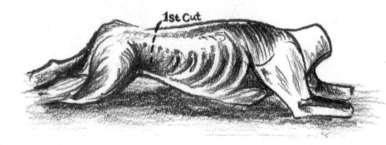

1st Cut

Ribs usually become stew and sausage meat, with the rest of the trim but some folks like to roast these ribs for their next meal, depending on the size and number of animals harvested.

The tenderloins and 'back-straps' are, in my opinion, the most prime pieces of meat on any large animal, and should be treated as such. They lie on either side of the spinal column, running horizontal to the spine, 'inside and out'.

Cut these out slowly and carefully, pulling lightly as you go. This is the most beautiful, succulent piece of meat so you don't want to allow any to go to waste.

If possible, watch someone who has experience with this before trying it yourself. But, there is certainly nothing to fear, but pulling away a well trimmed tenderloin is quite a prize.

They can be cooked whole, as an appropriately sized tenderloin roast, or sliced into medallions to become the 'filet mignon' cut. I include a recipe for stuffed venison tenderloin in this book. (Awesome!)

My Preferred method of breaking down a carcass:

Cut up between the hind legs and the spine, pulling the thighs outward. Be careful around the tenderloin area, not to damage the loin.

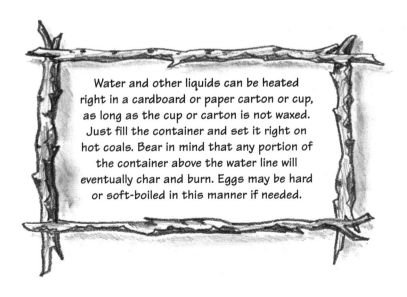

Water and other liquids can be heated right in a cardboard or paper carton or cup, as long as the cup or carton is not waxed. Just fill the container and set it right on hot coals. Bear in mind that any portion of the container above the water line will eventually char and burn. Eggs may be hard or soft-boiled in this manner if needed.

Saw through the spine with a meat or hacksaw. This leaves the hind legs hanging. Bring the front half to the butcher table, and proceed as stated above. Come back to the hind end last.

Separate the legs now, cutting along the spine. Now deal with each hind quarter individually. Before wrapping, briefly inspect each piece of meat. Cut away any that appears shot up or damaged.

Easy removal of hair that has come off the hide and stuck to the meat is easily done.

Using a handheld propane torch, pass quickly over said hair. It should burn up and disappear instantly. Use care not to burn or scorch the meat. Practice on a piece of scrap or two before going to better cuts.

Wrap in appropriately-sized servings (except for stew meat and other trimmings, which are well kept in a zipped plastic bag.) in butchers paper, and label as you go with a magic marker.

Be sure to include the year in which the game was harvested. Don't be afraid to use plenty of paper, to make sure the meat is well protected from freezer burn. The rate of deterioration in the freezer is slow, but I usually try to have it all used by the next hunting season to eliminate the hassle of rotating, and the risk of some being kept too long.

The next great danger is all the **myths and misconceptions** about how to cook game. Too many people think game will taste 'wild', or 'gamey'. This leads to overcooking, and using spices and sauces that cover the taste of the meat.

Wild game is rich and delicious if handled and prepared correctly. Many people experienced in hunting and cooking (and eating) will tell you, if you have any reservations about wild game – don't.

When handled and prepared correctly, wild game can, and will, rival any of its store-bought counterparts!

Cooking Wild Game

One of the most common mistakes is overcooking. Game is lower in fat, naturally, so once it is cooked past a certain point, it just becomes tough and dry.

An old friend of mine says it gets 'tougher than wang-leather.' I'm not sure what wang is (gamebird?), what it's fed or how it's raised, but it doesn't sound good.

Here are some **guidelines:**

Using a meat thermometer, pushed into a large cut of meat, but not touching a bone, if one exists: when the temp inside reaches 130° your meat is medium rare; 135° to 145° is medium; 150° is medium well; over 160° is well done.

I say the best is certainly not less than medium rare, and not ever much past medium. One exception is bear meat, which must always be cooked well done, to avoid trichinosis. (Also pork and chicken obviously need to be cooked thoroughly.)

Certainly, not all recipes here are expressly for wild game, but they could be. It is quite easy to substitute game for domestic meat, and vice versa. Play. Experiment. Enjoy yourself and those around you. Savor the flavor and satisfaction of well-prepared food. That is, after all, what it's all about.

Snapping Turtle

The snapping turtle has been a creature of varied reputation for years.

Adolescent boys are often told, to the amusement of the adults, tales of snappers and why they should never **skinny dip**.

Many folks who live near ponds or lakes, and are even vaguely knowledgeable of pond life and the Eco-cycle, are appreciative of its role as a pond scavenger of sorts.

It does feed on small fish, and even small birds that may be unlucky enough to land on the water at the wrong time. But it also cleans up a lot of other plant and animal materials that might otherwise go to waste. And it certainly is a very prolific creature. The indigenous peoples of North America were very reverent of this slow moving, but tough as nails creature.

Turtles are actually rather difficult to kill, or catch for that matter

in the water. Once on land, they're an easier target. I said easier ...
not easy.

Their shell is an incredible hiding spot, and their tails can move
powerfully, making a formidable weapon. And to be sure, they are
called snapping turtles for a good reason! They have been known
to bite onto a stick, or pole, when angry, and bite so hard that
they can support more than their own weight. And often, the jaws
can and will be capable of biting and holding, *even after the head
has been removed* from the turtle.

Certainly, this is an animal worthy of great respect, and valued
as a part of nature. But when harvested, they make great eating!
An elderly Swedish man that hangs around the lake I used to live
on has a method that he has used before, and swears by it. And
let me say this, from experience, when Bernie says a certain place,
method, or trick is good for catching a fish or turtle, I listen. That
old guy has this stuff down pat!

Bernie puts a piece of liver on a plain old hook – a big hook, and
ties the hook to a strong test line, which is tied to a fallen log, near
where the turtle is seen frequently. The liver is reportedly excellent
bait, and the strength and tenacity of the turtle will be sapped
over time, so it can be pulled in easier. Incidentally, the strong test
line he uses is real strong, more like thin rope. He says that some
folks like to join the rope and the log via an old tractor tire inner-
tube or bike tire. The elasticity helps to tire the turtle out (no pun
intended).

I've been told that turtles have seven different degrees of light
and dark meat! All I know is that when my Aunt Marie fixed this
years ago for me on the ranch, it was one of the best things I ever
had, although at the time it was definitely the strangest.

Many thanks to Marie and Bernie, this recipe is for you:

BAKED TURTLE

  2 tsp. salt
  1 tsp. black pepper
1/2 cup yellow cornmeal
  2 cups flour
  1 tsp. onion powder
1/2 cup crushed corn flakes
  1 tsp. paprika
1/4 cup vegetable oil
  1 turtle, cut into cubes/strips

Soak the meat overnight, or at least 4-5 hours, in lightly salted water. Remove from water, and drain. Pat lightly with towel to remove any excess water.

Combine other dry ingredients in a large mixing bowl. Roll pieces of turtle in mixture, and add to pan, with heated oil.

Brown lightly, giving each piece a turn or two as you go. Place meat either in a crock pot, on low heat for 2-3 hours, with a bit of water, or, over a fire, move over medium low coals, add a bit of water, cover, and, stirring occasionally, cook for 2 hours.

This is succulent meat, with lots of its own natural flavors, so try not to over-season.

EDIBLE WILD PLANTS AND MUSHROOMS
CATTAILS AS FOOD

Cattails can be harvested at different times of the year, and different parts of the plant can be used for different things. Just always make sure the surrounding area is free from pollution, and chemicals. (THAT is a sad thing to have to say.) I avoid harvesting near roadways or drainage ditches, instead opting to go to cleaner river backwaters.

In the spring of the year you can dig up the roots, and use the small bulbs like potatoes. Boil them until tender, dip them in butter and you have a great, unique addition to any meal.

In the summer months you can peel the stalks, by pulling down on the leaves, and breaking off the roots. This will expose the tasty inside of the stem. Wash this, and boil it up, or eat it raw.

It certainly would be an original addition to soups, or stews, and anywhere else you might otherwise use conventional potatoes.

They're also great sautéed! What a great, starchy, buttery flavor. And last, but not least, the roots may be dried, then pounded into a powder used as a type of flour, or used to supplement traditional wheat flour.

RAMPS or WILD LEEKS

The next time you are out in the woods, in spring and summer, keep an eye out for these wonderful little onions. Their mild flavor is delicious right out of the ground.

We often find them while searching for morels, as they are an early bloomer, often seen poking through the last of the snow, during warm, fast springs. They prefer the woods, and can often be found on the north sides of hills, especially if the ground is moist.

Their appearance is much like that of clusters of small lilies. The flat, oval green leaves will poke up from the ground 5-8 inches from the moist soil in which they grow. The stem extends a few inches into the ground, ending with the small bulb, about the size of a .22 shell, perhaps fatter.

A sharp stick, or screwdriver works well to aid in pulling them, since the bulbs can be a bit stubborn. Give the bulb a smell, and you'll know this one right away! If you can't wait to try this mild beauty, fear not. Wipe the dirt free, and enjoy. Otherwise, the entire plant may be used in soups, or other dishes.

Some reading that I have done about wild plants suggests that ramps have distinct medicinal properties.

It is recommended that you chop the leaves into a batch of chicken soup, to potentiate this cold and flu bug fighter. The same source also suggests that eating the raw bulbs of ramps may prevent heart disease.

Anyway, I just think they taste good.

DANDELION FLOWERS AS FOOD

These little buggers grow everywhere! The petals of the flower can be plucked off, and tossed in any salad, or other food dish that needs a splash of color. They are very rich in Beta-carotene, and so may be a cancer fighter.

I often prepare rice dishes while camping because of its portability, and health benefits. I sometimes sprinkle these petals over the rice, for color.

There's dandelion coffee, which is a bit bitter, but less so with sugar and also good for the liver (try saying that 5 times fast). Dry out some dandelion roots, then roast lightly, and powder. Add 1 teaspoon of the powder and one pinch of sugar, or a spot of honey, to 1 cup of hot water, and sip.

As for Dandelion wine, well ... that's my next book. I just need a little time to perfect the recipe.

MORELS AND SCRAMBLED EGGS

6	**fresh eggs**
About 1	**cup cleaned morel mushrooms**
1/4	**cup milk**
1/2	**lg. onion, diced**
1	**cup shredded cheese, cheddar**
3	**Tbs. butter, or margarine**

Scrambled eggs are obviously quite elementary. The aspect that really enhances them is the addition of one simple ingredient. Morel mushrooms.

These little treasures are found growing in the late spring, usually just as the lilac bushes start to bloom. Found on moist forest floors, they are often found within a close proximity to a dead elm tree. They are really easy to identify, because of their somewhat unique appearance. (I say SOMEWHAT unique, because there are a few species that do look like the morel, but are very nasty tasting.)

The best way to learn is to follow an experienced morel hunter, and be taught as you go. This might be the hardest part, since most 'mushroomers' that I've ever known are extremely protective of the locations that have provided for them in the past. (Since a good spot may produce for several years on end.)

Morels only recently have become available, commercially. If you wish to experience the taste, but not the cost of commercially-grown mushrooms, you may learn to identify them.

Always err on the side of caution, or nasty **poisoning** may occur. I live near a good state university that has helped me positively identify mushrooms before.

These experts (mycologists) have always been very happy to answer any questions I have about the mushrooms. And they're all too happy that someone will share an interest in their field. I'm told I'm quite a fungi.

Anyway, on with the recipe.

Heat the skillet, and add butter. Slice the mushrooms, (rinsed very well and sliced in half) and add to pan, with diced onions. Turn gently, while sautéing for two or so minutes.

In a bowl, break eggs; add milk, and spices. Whisk together

quickly. Add to the pan, and continue to cook, stirring occasionally. Just as eggs are getting done, add cheese to top layer of eggs, and put on a lid for a minute or two.

Serve with toast and fried potatoes, for a breakfast your guests won't soon forget! As a variation, you could prepare eggs without mushrooms, sauté them separately and serve them over the top of cooked eggs.

CHICKEN OF THE WOODS MUSHROOMS

This mushroom also goes by the name 'sulfur shelf', and 'chicken mushroom'.

This species is also known to be one of the **"unmistakable four"** mushrooms safe for consumption. Check with an expert anyway!

They are 'shelf' mushrooms, growing out from trees in a shelf-like manner. Their appearance in mid-fall is yellow, with a bizarre coloring scheme that makes them look as if they are covered in an orange dust.

I have harvested this species in chunks as large as 10 pounds, with one tree yielding 42 pounds of mushroom at once!

Cut from the tree with a large knife, holding a pail directly under the mushroom, to collect and save the 'blood' which is a rich golden-yellow color and is an excellent natural dye.

Wash off any dirt or other natural impurities. (Orange color is in mushroom, and can't be removed.)

Dice into pieces the size of a cherry pit, and simmer in a butter and chicken stock mixture. These mushrooms will take a long time to cook (30+ minutes).

I have found that I could just keep adding more and more butter, and the mushrooms would keep sucking it up. So I started adding the chicken stock, too.

I added them to a light cream sauce, and served them with wood-stove roasted pork tenderloin. None of us had ever actually had this kind of mushroom, but I had checked with a local expert, and was told that it was a semi-rare delicacy not commonly found in markets anywhere.

The flavor and texture of these fungi are almost exactly like that of … you guessed it! Chicken!

We were told that the genetic makeup of this mushroom is

almost exactly like that of animal protein, meat! Cool, or what?

P.S. – we also dehydrated some which worked well, but in subsequent years found another method that worked even better.

Prepare as above (dice, sauté) then put into ice cube trays and freeze. This freezes them in portions that are just about right for 1 small or 1/2 large serving!

One or two words of caution here:

ALWAYS consult with a professional before eating any wild mushroom. It can be a 'do-it-yourself' thing, and is for thousands of people, but you have to get some positive identification first. There are fungi out there that will make you very, very ill and some that will kill you.

Also, when and if you start to consume any wild mushrooms, remember this: eat any wild mushroom in small quantities first. Some peoples' bodies take longer to acclimate to some foods.

On a later expedition, we found an interesting shaggy mushroom growing from a tree. It was mostly a whitish color, and the ends of each 'shag' had started to turn a light rust color. This mushroom was nearly twelve inches in diameter. Upon identification, it proved to be a 'bearded tooth' or 'hedgehog' mushroom.

Its' appearance was very striking, for a mushroom! It is an edible, large tree mushroom, prepared in exactly the same manner as the fore-mentioned sulfur shelf mushroom.

These mushrooms are only a few of the many that, while walking through the woods, you can learn to identify and harvest. Be it a hunting trip or a leisurely stroll on a fall afternoon, these are forest delicacies!

But, and this bears repeating – ASK BEFORE YOU EAT! To not do so only proves why there aren't a lot of wild, renegade, risk-taking mushroom pickers out there.

Foraging for food should only be done with the means of absolute certain identification before consumption or use.

" I went to the woods to live, so
that I might live deliberately, and learn
what it had to teach me, so that I would
not, when it came time to die, learn that
I had not lived..."

~ *Henry D. Thoreau* ~

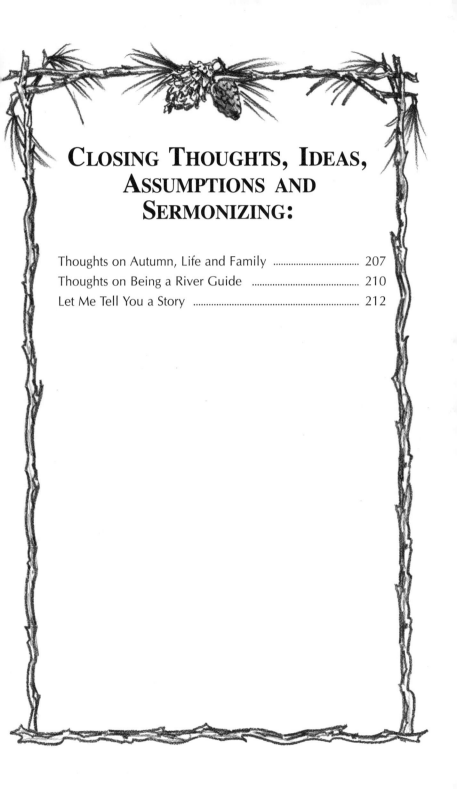

CLOSING THOUGHTS, IDEAS, ASSUMPTIONS AND SERMONIZING:

Thoughts on Autumn, Life and Family

It happens every year. I'll be sitting outside in the midst of another hot day; you know the kind … late summer, dusty and dry, the prairie grass turned into tall, dry sticks of tinder, the river running low, grasshoppers' grass-hopping around everywhere.

Then it happens, out of nowhere a breeze sneaks up, disguised as another hot summer wind, but this one feels subtly different. It has this faint tinge of coolness to it. A foreign property not felt for months. It's like a cool dust that settles on the back of your neck, telling of more changes to follow. Changes that will start small then grow exponentially clearer.

What will the next change be; trees along the river resigning their green color for the inevitability of autumn's yellows and golds? A sudden cold front that comes in late one night and finds all your windows open?

Fall is a time of change – a time of reflection. A time for realizing that the summer really is past and it's time to adjust to that other mode of living. That way of sucking the marrow out of the few warm days left. Time to take advantage of what's left of the passing warm season. Every nice day is now valued; every nice day is now numbered. We sense the impending cold white deeps of another winter.

As animals, we react in predictable ways. More sleep. More food. Flannel sheets and long-sleeved shirts start to sound appealing. Getting the most out of the garden harvest moves up the list of priorities. Children dart through the aisles of Wal-Mart excitedly grabbing up new supplies and new clothes for the first day back in school.

I see it in myself, too. I mow the lawn one last time wearing a sarcastic grin. I realize how good the gun oil smells as I clean the shotgun, with visions of a plenitude of pheasants the size of small turkeys flashing through my mind.

Hanging up the kayak for the year, I pull down my snow-boots and wonder if it's too soon to put the snow shovel next to the door. Hell, it's not even daylight savings time yet.

I step outside in the morning to sip coffee and enjoy the smell of the wet leaves on the grass. Fall even has it's own smell, it's own feel – and it comes in its own time.

It's part of the cycle of things, part of the way things have to work.

Realizing this brings to light deeper, more personal thoughts.

As seasons separate and mark divisions of the year, years separate and give clarity to the passing of life. With the passing of years comes closer the autumn of one's lifetime.

We all share the same seasons of nature simultaneously, but are subject to, sooner or later, the realization that our lives as a whole lie on a calendar somewhere that has a limited number of months and there is no renewal. There are no refills, no 'next years'.

I suspect that the breeze of change blows in softly and quietly there, too. I suspect that just as we all think in June that summer will last forever, the leaves always begin to turn too soon. But there is no stopping the pages of the calendar from turning.

All one can do is make the most of the days of spring and summer, and when fall finally comes, enjoy the warmth of the sun. Make the most of every day. The autumn of ones years should be golden. Take time to enjoy the smells and the colors, they are there for a reason. Enjoy the dirt on your hands and the fruits of your labors as you harvest the garden. Take your children's and grandchildren's hands now and walk with them through the falling leaves.

Slow or fast, winter always comes.

Thoughts on Being a River Guide

Stars glint overhead. The water gently laps against the pebble-strewn shore. Somewhere in the distance a coyote howls a wild greeting to the moon. I look around in the firelight and in this quiet moment, I know that I have done my job.

Tired paddlers share the last of their wine and a quiet period of contemplation as they stare into the glowing embers or gaze off into the night sky. A few are thinking with their eyes lightly closed, a subtle smile on their faces.

It has been another day on the river. Another day filled with the warmth of the sun, glimpses of turtles and fish and beaver. Another afternoon to view majestic bald eagles perched above us as we float by, and Blue Herons waiting for a fish to make a mistake. How many beavers did we see?

We feasted riverside on crab and Parmesan stuffed mushrooms. Then Caesar salad and garlic bread. Then grilled salmon and encrusted petite filet mignon. The garlic and shallots in red wine and beef stock reduction made a nice sauce. The s'mores were a hit for dessert.

My paddlers are ready to crawl into their tents and cozy in for the night. I reassure a young camper that the noisy screech owl about 25 yards into the trees is just an owl and nothing to worry about.

The guide will be the last one to bed – the first to rise. The stealthy shadow walking the camp perimeter in the middle of the night to make sure all is well and keep a thick log burning to start coffee when the sun comes up.

My fellow guide gives me a look and says he'll double-check the coolers before bed to ensure the raccoons will have no snacks. I respond that I will make sure the boats and gear are all secured.

Tired and sore we adjourn to our respective tents to sleep fast, well, and with one eye open. Storms can come up fast on the river and these folks have to know that they can count on us. Rely on our experience – trust our judgment.

I am proud to say that I work for Missouri River Expeditions. I am a river guide, just one of a team of men and women who lead others on kayaking and other outdoor adventures.

Let me Tell You a Story

Outdoor cooking can be fun and healthy. It can also be done on a shoestring budget. Take for example the following story.

It was mid-July, 1999, Saint Peter, Minnesota. I had just begun a new job, so my finances were quite tight. I read a story about a group of high school kids, all freshmen and sophomores, that were canoeing the Minnesota River on a summer science project. The expedition of 14 kids and two adult leaders, were making a journey of 335 ambitious miles. No easy deal, to be sure!

Now, figure in these facts: little or no experience, hot, humid days, and frequent severe storms at night. These guys had it rough!

I'm telling you, they missed camps, and over-paddled 2 days in a row, only to have to turn back, and paddle upstream to camp! Bad weather, mosquitoes, and a muddy river. Sound bad? Bad enough to bag it and call Mom and Dad for a ride home?

Not to these kids! They made the best of the situation and kept their chins up, and spirits high! The newspaper story said that the one thing they were missing most was a good meal, since they didn't cook well.

Now I hate to see anyone going through that much work with crappy food!

"Easy enough" I thought, I'll just take my little (big) bag of tricks (spice jars, stocks, utensils, Dutch Oven , 4 foot by 4 foot grill, and assorted mixes and sauces) down to the river, meet them, and show them how to improvise with what they had.

I would prove my theory that with a dash of ingenuity and a few basic spices, you can make potluck out of most anything. I got to the river and found that they didn't have anything. Peanut butter, a bit of jelly, and canned chili. Ummm, no. I mean, you've gotta have something to work with.

I ran to the grocery store quick, and spent $28.00 on groceries. I got country-style pork ribs (16 pieces) and chicken (16 pieces), with 25 ears of sweet corn, and over 1 1/2 cases of cold soda. I figured it out later ... $1.75 per person, with soda left over!

I lit the fire, while they and their leaders set up camp. A short time later they had barbequed chicken and ribs, Dutch Oven-roasted sweet corn and cold caffinated, carbonated, appreciated soda. The end result was many satisfied, tired, dirty young travelers.

They told me crazy stories about their adventures while eating vigorously, said their "thank you's", and went softly to bed. I packed up my things and went home to clean up, feeling awesome!

My point here is that if you want to, you can feed many for little, just as easy on the open fire as you can indoors and somehow it always tastes just a little better that way.

By the way, if any of those kids, or instructors are reading this, hats off to you! You guys made a tough trip and learned a lot, I'm sure.

It's adults like that, who take the time and energy to give to and teach our kids like that, that will produce the next generation of outdoorsmen (and women) that will appreciate, utilize, and care for our green world. They were taught the rewards of hard work and perseverance. Something we desperately need!

Amen.

Notes:

_____

_____

_____

_____

_____

_____

_____

_____

_____

_____

_____

_____

_____

_____

_____

_____

Notes:

_____

_____

_____

_____

_____

_____

_____

_____

_____

_____

_____

_____

_____

_____

_____

Notes:

_____

_____

_____

_____

_____

_____

_____

_____

_____

_____

_____

_____

_____

_____

_____

_____

Notes:

Notes:

Won't you join us for a retreat or adventure excursion?

We don't need a special reason to get away to kayak, camp, or simply spend time in an environment apart from the busy, pressure-filled world of daily life. In our time apart, we find that adventure, discovery, and peaceful feelings come naturally. They stimulate new thought patterns, help us gain insights and evoke ideas that wouldn't come as easily in another environment.

> • Getting away from work's hustle and bustle gives business groups or teams the opportunity and time to think, learn and plan together, to focus their efforts, to concentrate, to work together without interruption...

- Getting away from the routine helps us re-connect; being apart, in nature leads us to different ways to re-build and strengthen relationships...

- Getting away from the expected opens the door to the unexpected; it allows us to fill our heads with new thoughts, to think in terms of possibilities instead of limitations...

- Getting away brings a new perspective on how we can re-define and refine. It helps us look at old issues from a new vantage point and helps us feel less stress. We think differently and return re-energized, ready to address old issues with new ways of thinking.

For over a dozen years, we've designed retreats that support and supplement the training and coaching we provide for business clients. We design special retreats to help businesses and individuals meet a variety of needs.

Now we have adventure weekends specifically for families...parent/child and grandparent/grandchild retreats are wonderful experiences. Helping people connect with others is a North Country goal because it is a natural result of working and playing together outdoors. We'd love to work with you to design a retreat, and adventure excursion, or a family get-away experience.

For more information on business retreats, family excursions, and adventure weekends, please contact

North Country Enterprises at:
(605) 335-3224 or **(605) 661-0211**
Or visit us on the web at
www.gonorthcountry.org

Tony Kellar lives in Mission Hill, SD with his son TJ and their dog, Buck. They are all avid campers, hikers, hunters and paddlers.

His summers are spent working for Missouri River Expeditions guiding kayak and canoe trips all over the US, as well as camping and paddling with friends and family.

He also works with his father, Jim Kellar, designing and facilitating retreats and seminars for businesses, groups, and families. He also gives cooking and camping demonstrations, speaking at conventions, schools, and outdoor events.

His deep and abiding love and respect for the outdoors and his focus on hospitality have made him a favorite of people who seek ways to more fully experience nature. He is a natural teacher and a perpetual student.